Canva

From Beginner to Pro

Master Canva Step by Step to Create Professional Designs for Graphics, Social Media, Presentations, Videos, Marketing Materials, and More

Jaxon Strathmore

TABLE OF CONTENTS

CHAPTER 1

INTRODUCTION TO CANVA

What is Canva?

Canva is an online design platform that lets anyone make a lot of different kinds of visual content without having to know a lot about graphic design. It's known for having an easy-to-use interface that lets people, businesses, and groups use it without any technical knowledge. Canva has tools and templates that can help you make designs that look professional quickly and easily, no matter how much design experience you have or how little it's been used before. Since it came out in 2013, the platform has become one of the most famous design tools in the world. It works with a freemium model, which means that many features are available for free, but users can get access to more premium features, templates, and elements by subscribing to Canva Pro or Canva for Teams.

Key Features of Canva

1. **Templates:** Canva has thousands of samples of already-designed templates for social media posts, presentations, resumes, posters, business cards, invites, and more. There are professional designs on these templates, and users can change the colors, fonts, pictures, and layouts to make them fit their needs.
2. **Drag-and-Drop Interface:** One of the best things about Canva is its drag-and-drop interface, which means you don't need to know how to code or use complicated tools. It's easy and simple for users to make things because they can just pick out elements like text, images, shapes, and icons and place them on their design canvas.
3. **Media Library:** Canva has a huge library of design elements, such as stock photos, drawings, fonts, shapes, icons, audio and video clips, and more. A lot of these parts are free, but you have to pay for a contract to get to the paid ones.
4. **Collaboration:** Canva lets multiple people work on the same design at the same time using real-time teamwork. This is especially helpful for teams or projects that need input from a lot of people. Commenting, sharing designs through links and giving jobs like editors or viewers are all collaborative features.
5. **Versatility:** The tool can be used for a wide range of purposes, from personal to business. People can use Canva to make personal projects like picture collages, greeting cards, and event invitations, and businesses can use it for branding, marketing, and promotional materials.
6. **Mobile and Desktop Compatibility:** Canva has a web app and mobile tools for both Android and iOS devices. Cross-platform compatibility makes sure that users can view and change their designs from any device, like a computer, tablet, or phone.
7. **Canva Pro:** Canva Pro gives users access to more features, such as endless storage; the ability to make brand kits with custom fonts, colors, and logos; advanced design tools; premium templates; and access to a larger media library.

Why People Use Canva

Canva is popular because it is easy to use and understand. Professional design programs like Adobe Photoshop and Illustrator usually need a lot of technical know-how and time to use. Canva, on the other hand, is made to be easy for anyone to use. This makes it a great choice for small businesses, teachers, students, marketers, and anyone else who wants to make content that looks good without paying a designer. A small business owner, for instance, could use Canva to design social media graphics or promotional flyers without having to hire someone else to do it. For example, a student could use it to make a show for a class project that is interesting to look at.

Common Use Cases

1. **Social Media Content:** A lot of people use Canva to make posts, stories, banners, and ads that work on Instagram, Facebook, Twitter, LinkedIn, and TikTok. Its templates make sure that designs are the right size for every device.
2. **Marketing and Branding:** Canva helps companies keep their brand consistent across all of their materials, from business cards and brochures to logos and ads. One more thing that makes this process easier is the brand kit option in Canva Pro.
3. **Educational Materials:** Canva is frequently used by teachers and students to design worksheets, infographics, presentations, and posters for the classroom.
4. **Events and Personal Projects:** A lot of people use Canva to make invitations, greeting cards, picture collages, and other personalized designs for holidays, weddings, birthdays, and other events.
5. **Video Editing:** Canva's video editing tools aren't as advanced as those in specialized software, but it still lets users make simple videos with music, transitions, and text overlays.

Advantages of Canva

- **Ease of Use:** The platform's design makes it easy to use, even for novices.
- **Affordability:** The free version has a lot of features, and the paid plans aren't too expensive when compared to professional design software.
- **Variety of Options:** Canva has thousands of templates and design elements, so it can meet the needs of a wide range of businesses.
- **Cloud-Based:** Because Canva is in the cloud, users can edit their projects from anywhere and quickly share them with other people.
- **Customizability:** Canva has templates that are already made, but users can start from scratch and make their own designs.

Limitations

Canva is flexible and strong, but it's not as good as professional design tools in some ways. For example, it might not have as many ways to change things and be as precise as tools like Adobe Creative Suite. Canva's tools might not be enough for difficult projects for experienced designers. Canva does, however, have more than enough features for most everyday design needs.

Understanding Canva's Interface

The interface of Canva is designed to be easy to use, so even people who have never designed anything before can make professional-looking graphics with no trouble. It's split up into different areas, and each one has a specific job to do. This makes it easy for users to connect with the platform. The interface is designed to make all the tools you need easy to find, whether you're making a simple graphic for social media or a presentation with many pages.

The Homepage

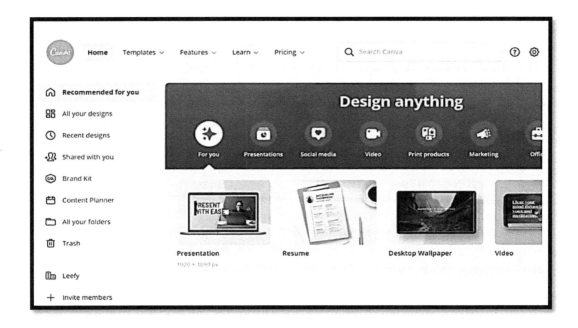

The **home page** is where you start when you first log in. There is a search bar at the top where you can put in what you want to make. For example, if you need an Instagram post template, all you have to do is type in the keywords, and Canva will show you hundreds of choices that fit your needs. **Templates** have tens of thousands of designs that are grouped into groups that make it easy to find what you need. **Features** show you photos, icons, print media, apps, and other things that can help you design what you need. There are blog posts, short lessons, and full courses on **Learn** that can help you learn more about design. **Pricing** tells you how to become a Pro or get an account for a nonprofit. There are many types of sections below the search bar, such as **"Social Media," "Presentations," "Videos," "Posters,"** and more. By assisting you in quickly finding templates that are suited to your needs, these categories are meant to save you time. For instance, if you choose "Presentations," you'll see ready-made designs in the normal presentation size that come with slide layouts that you can change.

Canva's Side Menu

You have an extra **Home** button in case you need to reset after going deep into something. Then there's **Your projects**, where you can arrange and find your designs. Make folders to keep things organized, and let other people work on the same designs or files with you. **Templates** give you access to tens of thousands of designs that can help you get ideas. **Recommended** tab shows you things that you might like based on your designs. The **Shared with You** page makes it easy to find designs that you will work on together. Any designs, pictures, or movies you've deleted are in the **Trash**.

The Design Dashboard

The first thing you see when you start a new project is the **design dashboard**. This is where the magic happens. This is the main area where you work on your designs and make changes to them. The **canvas**, which shows the design itself, takes up most of the screen. The canvas is very interactive; it's easy to drag and drop pieces, change their size, and move them around. No matter if you're editing text, pictures, or shapes, everything takes place right on the canvas, so you can see the changes as they happen.

The Toolbar

You can see the **toolbar** above the canvas. It changes based on what you're working on. For example, if you pick some text, the toolbar will show you ways to change the font, size, color, alignment, and even add effects like shadows or outlines. To crop, resize, flip, or change the transparency of a picture, the toolbar will have tools for those tasks. This dynamic toolbar makes sure that you can always get to all the tools you need without making the area too crowded.

The Sidebar

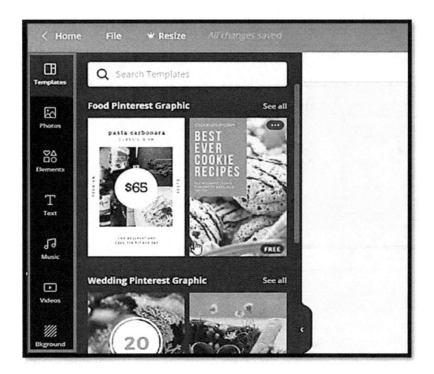

The **sidebar**, which is on the left side of the screen, helps you find things you need for your design. This area has several tabs, and each one does a different thing. On the first tab, "**Templates**," you can look through thousands of layouts that have already been created and are specific to the type of project you are working on. The next tab is **Elements**, which has a huge collection of shapes, icons, images, charts, frames, and grids that you can use to organize your design. When you click on the **Uploads** tab, you can add your own photos, videos, or audio clips. This way, you can add personal or unique content to your designs. The **Text** tab lets you choose from different text styles and pre-made font choices. This makes it simple to add headlines and body text that stand out. You can also look through Canva's huge library of stock images in the **Photos** tab. For the background of your design, you can choose from a variety of colors, patterns, and images in the **Backgrounds** tab. The **bottom panel** is great for projects like slideshows and ebooks that have a lot of pages. You can see thumbnails of each page here, which lets you move between them or change the order of them. It's also easy to copy or remove pages from this panel, so you have full control over how your project flows and is organized. One great thing about Canva is that you can use **drag-and-drop** to make things without having to know how to use complicated tools or code. Like, to add an icon to your design, all you have to do is pick it up from the Elements tab and drag it onto the page. It's as easy as clicking and dragging to change the size, rotation, or location of an icon once it's there. This way of doing things makes Canva very easy for newbies to use while still giving experienced designers enough freedom. The power to **customize every element** of the interface is also very important. Canva has tools that let you make the design truly yours, whether you're working with text, images, or shapes. For example, you can change the style, size, and color of text boxes to suit your tastes. You can also change the spacing and placement, and you can add effects like neon glows or shadows. Canva has built-in tools that let you crop images, add filters, and change the color and contrast of images. You can change the size, color, and rotation of shapes and lines to make them fit your plan. Canva also lets people work together in real time, which is great for group projects. You can let other people see or change your design by clicking the "Share" button in the upper right corner of the screen. You can give people roles like "Editor" or "Viewer" with this feature, making sure that everyone has the right amount of access. People working on the project can leave comments right on the design, which makes it easy to share thoughts and make the project better as a whole. The interface makes it easy to export or share your work once you're done with your design. The "Share" button can also be used to send files in PNG, JPG, PDF, MP4, and GIF formats, among others. You could download the design to your phone or computer, share it on social media sites, or even print it through Canva's printing services, depending on your needs.

CHAPTER 2

GETTING STARTED WITH CANVA

Creating an Account

Step 1: Visit the Canva Website or Download the App

Get to the official Canva page at www.canva.com to start. If you have a smartphone or computer, you can also get the Canva app from the app store for that device. Since the app is available for both iOS and Android, it should work on most devices.

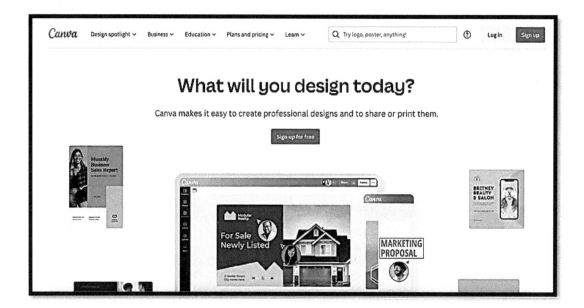

Step 2: Click on the "Sign Up" or "Get Started" Button

There is a big button on the Canva homepage or app starting screen that says "**Sign Up**," "**Get Started**," or "**Try Canva Free**." If you click this button, you'll be taken to the registration page where you can start creating your account.

Step 3: Choose a Sign-Up Method

Canva gives users a choice of ways to make an account, so they can suit their needs. Here's how to sign up:

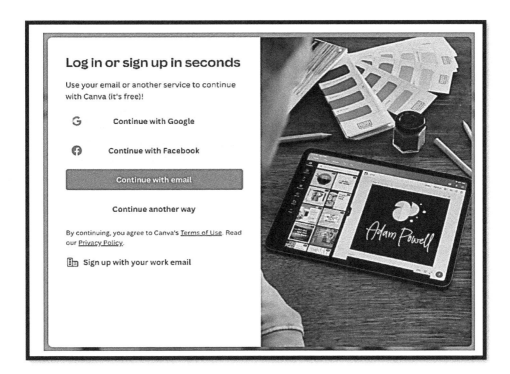

1. **Email Address**: This is the way people have always done it. You will need to make a password and give a current email address. If you want a Canva account that isn't connected to any other site, this is the best choice.
2. **Google Account**: It only takes a few clicks to sign up for Canva if you already have a Gmail account. This way is helpful because you don't have to remember another password.
3. **Facebook Account**: You can also sign up for Canva with your Facebook information. If you choose this choice, Canva will connect your account to your Facebook profile, which will make it easy to log in.
4. **Apple ID**: Apple users can sign up with an Apple ID, which is another safe and easy way to do it.

Each way has its own benefits, so which one you choose will rely on your personal taste and how well you want to connect to other platforms.

Step 4: Enter Your Details

If you want to use your email address to sign up, you'll need to fill out a form. This is what you'll usually give:

- **Full Name**: Type in your first and last name as you want them to show up on your Canva profile.
- **Email Address**: Give a valid email address that you can access because Canva may give you important messages, updates, or instructions on how to reset your password.
- **Password**: To keep your information safe, pick a strong password that includes numbers, capital and lowercase letters, and special characters.

Most of this information is taken from your current account when you sign up through Google, Facebook, or Apple. This saves you time.

Step 5: Agree to the Terms and Conditions

Canva will ask you to agree to their terms of service and privacy policy before you can move forward. You should read these quickly to get a sense of how Canva handles your information and what to expect from their site. To move forward, check the box or click the "**Confirm**" button when you're ready.

Step 6: Verify Your Email Address (If Required)

Canva may ask you to confirm your email address before they let you finish the signup process. If this step is needed, you'll get an email with a link to do it. Open the email and click on the link inside. This will take you to Canva, where your account is now fully enabled.

Step 7: Choose Your Account Type

Once you've made an account, Canva will ask you to describe how you want to use the site. Usually, these are the choices:
- **Personal Use**: This is great for people who want to make designs for things like greetings, resumes, or social media posts.
- **Business**: Made for businesses and workers who need branding tools, marketing materials, and ways to work together?
- **Education**: Made for teachers and students, with tools for projects and tasks in the classroom.
- **Nonprofit**: This is for groups that want to make promotional materials to raise money or recognition.

By letting you pick an account type, Canva can customize your experience by giving you the right templates, tools, and features.

Step 8: Explore Canva's Free and Paid Plans

Canva may offer you the chance to upgrade to Canva Pro, Canva for Teams, or Canva for Education after you have set up your account. The free version has a lot of useful tools, but upgrading gives you access to paid templates, a huge media library, and extra features like brand kits and content planning. You can start with the free plan if you're not sure and then upgrade if you need to.

Logging In After Account Creation

It's easy to log in after creating an account. You can enter your email address and password, Google, Facebook, or Apple ID when you go back to the Canva website or open the app and click "**Log In**." If you choose to save your login information, a lot of browsers and gadgets can do it for you so you can get to it faster.

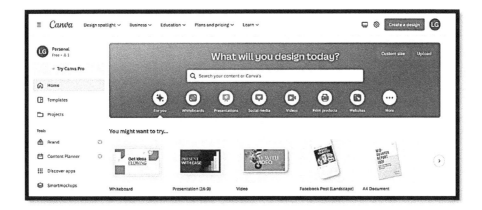

Using the Mobile Version of Canva

I'd now like to talk a little about the Canva app for phones. And since most people now do jobs and everyday things on their phones instead of computers, you should also set up this app. You can log in to both the PC and web versions of Canva with the same information. All of your designs uploads, photos, and logos will be synced across once you do this. This means that you can view anything you make on your computer through the app on your phone. Just a few small things are different, and the website doesn't have all of the tools that the app does. The screen size is the only clear change between them. At our desks and computers, we can see a lot more and make plans for bigger projects. The small screen on your phone makes it easy to get designs, organize things, and post to social media while you're out and about. You can get the Canva app for your phone from either the Google Play Store or the Apple App Store. It's likely to be an ad at the top of the page. Pick **Canva**, and then use your Canva login to log in.

10

Then it will open on your phone and show you this screen:

The PC version of Canva is a little different from the mobile version in the ways below:
- Click on the **little purple circle** in the bottom right corner to draw. The main menu is not to the left but across the bottom.

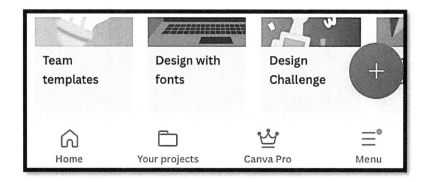

- All of the template's parts are at the bottom when creating, not the top:

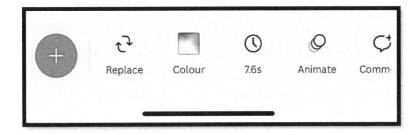

Tap the little purple circle in the bottom left corner of the screen while you're designing to get to the elements. A white circle with a number in a square inside it is on the right side of the screen. This lets you see all of your pages at once:

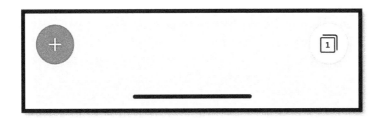

Making a Profile in Canva and Start Design

1. Sign in to your account on Canva.
2. In the upper right part of the screen, click on the "**Profile**" icon.
3. Press the "**Create Profile**" button.
4. Type in your name, email address, and other contact information.
5. Put up a profile picture and a cover photo.
6. Add a short bio about yourself.
7. Press the "**Save**" button.

You can start making content as soon as you finish making your profile. To do this, click "**Create**" and pick the kind of content you want to create. Canva lets you make many kinds of content, like posts for social media, slideshows, flyers, and more. If you're going to write something, give it a title and a short description. The title should be short and clear, and the description should help people understand what the material is about.

Profile Settings

Edit account name and purpose for using Canva

1. Go to **Settings** from the home page. Check that you're on the **Account** tab.
2. Type in a new name by clicking "**Edit**" next to your name.
3. To finish, click **Save**.
4. To change what you use Canva for, scroll down and look for **what will you be using Canva for?**
5. Click on the dropdown and select an option. The changes will be saved immediately.

If you want your account name to show up in Canva emails (for example, when you invite team members to a design or share it), you should only use letters and not numbers or special characters.

Upload or Change Profile Photo

1. In the upper right part of the home page, click on your profile picture.
2. Move your mouse over the current photo. A camera icon will appear. Press it.
3. Pick the file you want to send from your phone or tablet, then click "**Open**." Your profile picture will be changed automatically after the upload is done.

Setting up your Creator profile page

You get a public profile where people can see your assets and templates as a Canva Creator. To promote your business, make changes to your page's information.

1. To get to your Account Settings, click the **gear icon** in the upper right part of the home page.
2. Select "**Public Profile**" from the side panel.
3. Edit your details. When you fill out your Canva profile URL, only lowercase letters and no spaces should be used.
4. To finish, click "**Save changes.**"

There is a link to your profile at the top of the page that you can click to see it.

Can't update your display name or URL?

Your display name and the name of your URL can't be the same. Give each one a different name.

Update Public Profile Photo

To change your profile picture, go to the homepage and click on your **account icon**. Then, click on your account icon again to add your picture.

Public Profile Page Not Available

Make sure you're in the brand of either Creator or Contributor.

1. Click the **account icon** in the upper right area of the Canva home page.
2. Scroll down until you see "**Switch team**." It shows all the brands and teams you're a part of.
3. Check for the name of your Contributor brand. If there's no ✔ next to it, click to switch to it. The page will then refresh.

If you can't see your Contributor brand under **Switch Teams**, make sure you're logged in to the right account.

CHAPTER 3
DESIGN ESSENTIALS

Creating a New Design

You will need to open a new canvas to work on a project. You can do two things.

1. Start from scratch to create your canvas. Click on the blue "**Create a Design**" button in the upper left corner. Pick "**Custom Size**" and enter the width and height you want.
2. **Choose a pre-made canvas.** If you need to make a project for a certain reason, like a Facebook ad, you will need to make images that are a certain size. It's simple to do this. Enter the graphic's name or scroll down the list until you find it. Then click "**Create a design**." There are whiteboards for pins, email headers, restaurant menus, and just about anything else you could need.

Choosing the Right Template

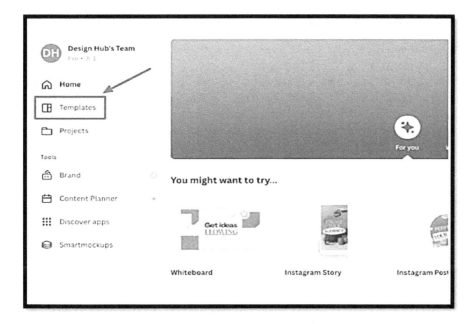

Canva's templates are pre-designed layouts that serve as inspiration for your own work. They have things like pictures, text boxes, graphics, and placeholders that are carefully placed to keep the design balanced. With templates, you don't have to start from scratch, which makes them especially useful for people who aren't good at design or don't have much time. Picking the right template will make sure that your content looks good and works with the platform. For example, a business presentation needs a clean, formal style, while a birthday invitation might need bright colors and fun fonts. Templates also make sure that the right sizes and formats are used for different platforms, like Instagram posts, YouTube thumbnails, and written materials.

How to Choose the Right Template

Step 1: Define Your Purpose

Before you choose a template, you should know what you want your design to do. Think about these:
- What am I making? Do I want it to be a resume, flyer, poster, chart, or something else?
- Who is my audience? Who are you creating for? Are they business clients, students, friends, or the general public?
- How is this design going to be used? Is it going to be posted online on social media, shown in a meeting, or printed out and given out?

The types of templates you should look into will depend on how you answer these questions. The templates in Canva are grouped by type, which makes it easy to find ones that work for you. **As an example:**
- For social media, you'll find templates for Instagram posts, Facebook covers, and Pinterest pins.
- For professional use, explore templates for business cards, presentations, and letterheads.
- For personal projects, Canva offers options like photo collages, wedding invitations, and party flyers.

Step 2: Use the Search Bar

Once you know what you want to do, you can use Canva's search bar to find templates that fit your needs. If you need a design for an event, for example, type "event flyer" or "party invitation," and Canva will show you a list of templates that match your search. This way, you won't have to scroll through options that aren't relevant. **You can also use terms that are related to themes, styles, or colors in the search bar. As an example:**
- Look for a "**minimalist presentation**" if you want something cutting-edge and simple.
- Use terms like "**Christmas card**" or "**summer party flyer**" for projects that are holiday- or season-themed.

Step 3: Choose the Right Dimensions

Canva templates are already the right size for certain platforms or file types, so you don't have to make any changes to your design to make it fit. This step is especially important for digital projects because the wrong size can make your content look bad. **As an example:**
- **Social Media**: For social media, Instagram posts need to be 1080x1080 pixels square, while Pinterest pins need to be 1000x1500 pixels vertical.
- **Print Projects**: A4 or letter-size paper is often used for posters and flyers, and standard card sizes are used for business cards.

Choose a "Custom Size" option to make a blank canvas with the exact dimensions you need, or filter templates by size if you have specific needs.

Step 4: Consider Your Style

Your message and viewers should fit with the style of your template. Canva has a lot of different styles, from bright and bold to simple and clean.

To pick the right one:
- **Look for Color Themes**: For example, a bright and fun template might work for a call to a kids' party, while a serious report would be better with a more subdued color scheme.
- **Assess Font Choices**: Event posters look great with templates that use big, fancy fonts, but official presentations and resumes look better with more traditional fonts.
- **Focus on Layout**: For business projects, simple layouts with lots of white space work best, while for creative projects, templates with lots of moving pictures work best.

Step 5: Preview Multiple Options

Look at a few different templates before deciding on one. When you click on a template, it will open in Canva's designer. From there, you can look more closely at its structure and parts. Think about it:
- Is there the right amount of text and pictures in this template for my needs?
- Are the placeholder elements easy to customize?
- Does the overall style align with my vision?

See how different templates look before you buy them to find the best one for your project.

Step 6: Prioritize Customization

Templates should still feel special to your project even though they are meant to save time. Look for templates that can be changed in a number of ways. You can change almost everything about a template in Canva, like the colors, fonts, images, and layouts. But you might need to make more changes to some templates than to others in order to make them work for you.

As an example:
- If you only have two photos to add, it might be hard to change a template that has spaces for five pictures.
- If you need to match a certain color scheme or style, it might take longer to change templates with complicated graphics.

Pick a template that you can easily change but that will still give your design a strong base.

Common Mistakes to Avoid

1. **Choosing a Template Based Solely on Appearance**

The way the template looks is important, but how well it works is even more important. You might waste time and effort on a beautiful template that doesn't work with your content or goals.

2. **Ignoring the Target Audience**

If the design style doesn't match what the audience expects, it can hurt your message. For example, putting together a business report with a funny template might not come across as professional.

3. **Overlooking Template Dimensions**

If you use the wrong size for your tool or medium, you might end up with pixels, cropping problems, or bad print quality. Always check the measurements twice before moving on.

4. **Skipping Customization**

If you use a template without making any changes, you might end up with a boring design that doesn't have any style. Adding your brand colors or changing the fonts are just a few of the small changes that can make a big difference.

Practical Example: Selecting a Social Media Template

Say you're making an Instagram post to tell people about a sale this summer. In Canva's search bar, type "summer sale Instagram post" to begin. The platform will show different templates, which usually have big fonts, bright colors, and seasonal pictures like beach or sun scenes. Look at a few choices and pick the one that fits the tone of your brand. If your business is simple, choose a design that is cleaner and has fewer colors. If it's more fun, choose a template with animated icons or bright gradients that stand out. After picking a template, you can make it your own by adding your image, changing the colors to match your brand, and adding text that is related to your sale.

Saving Your Design and Other Options

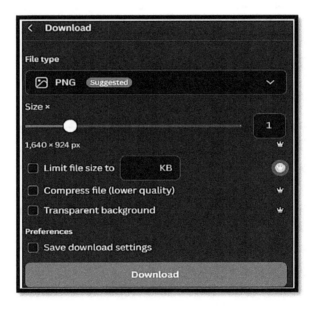

You only need to save your design when you're done with it. You're almost at the end of your journey. Click the "**Save**" button in the upper left corner of the page to keep your design. Then, click "Download," pick the type of file, and click "**Download**" at the bottom to send it. Wait a little while, and you'll be done! You can also share your design on Canva in other ways, such as but not limited to, the ones below:
- Saving the design to Google Drive or Dropbox.
- Sharing the design directly to different social media platforms.
- Sending a shareable link to others for collaboration.
- Ordering prints straight from Canva which will eventually arrive at your doorstep.

Exploring the Design or Editing Tools

There are different groups of Canva's design tools that are grouped to help with different parts of the design process. You can change text, images, colors, layouts, and other things with these tools to make your artistic ideas come to life. You can use the tools for any type of design project, like a social media post, a business show, or an invitation.

Let us help you get used to the design or editing tools before you start editing. This will make sure that everything goes smoothly as you work. Canva will take you to the Design Page after you pick a template or design. On the left side of this page, you'll see a Toolbar that has the following items:

A. Design

You can use design templates that you can change to fit your canvas, or you can choose from Styles, which gives you font sets, color palettes, or blends of fonts and color palettes to use in your design.

B. Elements

This tool makes it easy to get to thousands of different design features. Some of these design elements are stickers, photos, videos, music, charts, polls, frames, mockups, an AI image generator, and shapes. Also, the search bar makes it easy to find anything you need for the design. To change a design feature, all you have to do is select it. A small toolbar will then show up on top of the page. You can change this element by changing its color, adding a border, changing its shape, cropping it, rotating it, changing how transparent it is, moving it around, and even choosing an animation for it.

C. Text

There's no doubt that every design needs some writing. Just tap on the "Text" bar to add text. You can add a title, a subheading, or body text. You can change the text in the same way that you can change the design features. To change text, all you have to do is tap on it, and a small horizontal menu will show up on top of the page. You can change the text's color, typeface, style, and case, as well as its size, alignment, use of text effects, placement, and animation.

D. Uploads

With this feature, you can upload photos, videos, audio files, or gifs from your computer that you want to use in your design. You could also use Google Drive, Dropbox, or Google Photos to add items.

E. Draw

This function gives you more freedom to make your design however you want. Draw lets you add life to your design by using digital drawing tools like a pen, pencil, marker, and eraser. You can also change the color of the drawing tools, as well as their size and transparency. If you tap on an element or word, you may also see other editing tools. A smaller menu will appear on top of an element or text after you tap on it. If you want to use other popular editing tools, like copy, paste, duplicate, delete, comment, link, or lock, you can.

Understanding Other Tools

1. **Image Editing Tools** for working with photos and graphics.
2. **Color Tools** for selecting and applying color schemes.
3. **Alignment and Layout Tools** for organizing your design elements.
4. **Effects and Filters** for enhancing visuals.
5. **Animation Tools** for dynamic, interactive designs.
6. **Collaboration Features** for team projects.

All of these tools work perfectly with Canva's design center and can be reached from the toolbar, side panels, or context menus.

Image Editing Tools

Images are often the most important part of a design, and Canva's tools for editing images let you change photos and drawings to fit your style. Some important features are:

- **Upload and Insert Images**: You can use their large library of stock photos and drawings or upload pictures from your computer.
- **Resizing and Cropping**: You can change the size and shape of images to draw attention to certain parts or make them fit into frames and grids.
- **Filters and Adjustments**: Canva has filters that are already made to change the tone or mood of your photos. You can also change color, contrast, saturation, and other things by hand.
- **Background Remover**: This is a paid tool that lets you get rid of an image's background with just one click. It's great for making cutouts or transparent overlays.
- **Frames and Grids**: You can drag and drop pictures into frames or grids to make organized layouts or one-of-a-kind shapes.

Color Tools

The colors you use have a big impact on the mood and message of your design. The color tools in Canva make it simple to use and change color schemes:

- **Color Picker**: You can use the color choices to give text, backgrounds, or shapes solid colors. For accuracy, you can enter hex numbers or choose colors that are already there.
- **Brand Colors**: Canva Pro users can make a brand kit that stores their company's colors so they can be used quickly in all designs.
- **Gradients**: To give backgrounds or parts a modern and lively look, add gradient overlays on top of them.
- **Transparency**: Change an element's opacity to add minor effects or layer them.

Alignment and Layout Tools

For designs to look balanced and professional, they need to be laid out and aligned correctly.

Canva has tools that can help you arrange and line up elements:
- **Grid Lines and Snapping**: As you move things around in Canva, alignment guides appear to help you put things in the right place.
- **Group and Ungroup**: Place several items in a group to move or resize them as a single unit.
- **Arrange and Layering**: Put things in a different order to move them forward or backward.
- **Resize Tool**: Are you a Canva Pro user? If so, the resize tool lets you change the size of your design to fit different forms, like turning an Instagram post into a Facebook banner.

Effects and Filters

There are effects and filters in Canva that can make your designs more creative and professional:
- **Image Effects**: To give photos a unique look, use effects like duotone, vignette, or pixelate.
- **Text Effects**: To make a word stand out, use effects like neon, glitch, or shadow.
- **Advanced Filters**: Canva lets you change certain parts of a picture, like its tint or temperature, to have more control over how it looks.

Animation Tools

Canva's animation tools let you bring your designs to life for projects that need to move:
- **Element Animation**: You can add animations like fade, slide, or bounce to certain elements, like text or images.
- **Page Transitions**: You can add changes between pages in designs with more than one page to make the visual story flow smoothly.
- **Export Options**: You can save animated designs as videos or GIFs that you can then share on Instagram or in presentations.

Collaboration Features

Canva has tools for team projects that make collaboration easy:
- **Real-Time Editing**: More than one person can work on the same design at the same time, and changes are seen right away.
- **Commenting**: Members of the team can leave feedback or suggestions directly on the design by leaving comments.
- **Role Assignments**: To limit who can see what, give people roles like "Editor" or "Viewer."

Setting Up Folders Your Designs

In Canva, you can make groups to organize your designs into different areas of your work or personal life. It's easy to find the things you've shared and see your newest designs on the "**Your Projects**" tab. This is on the left side of the screen, next to the Home tab.

Here's the order of the parts on this page:
- Recent
- Folders
- Designs
- Images
- Videos

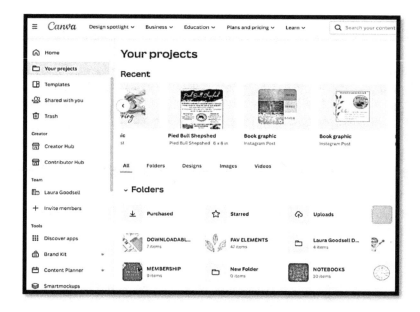

At the bottom of the page is everything you've shared or made. It's the hub of your account and the best place to get to everything.

Creating Folders

Your account already has three folders. These are them:

- **Purchased** – This section holds everything you've bought that wasn't included in your Pro subscription.
- **Starred** – It holds any elements or pictures you've liked and want to use later.
- **Uploads** – It holds all the photos and videos you add to your account.

You get an unlimited number of folders in both the Pro and Free versions, not just the three that were mentioned. You can call them anything you want. To make a new folder, follow these steps:

1. In the top right corner, click on the cross. That will bring up a menu with the words "**Add new**":

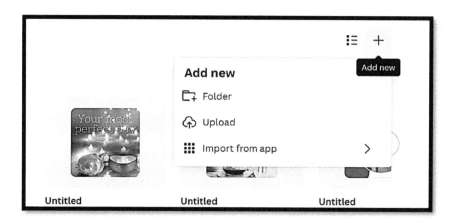

2.   Press on the folder icon.
3.   Name your folder.

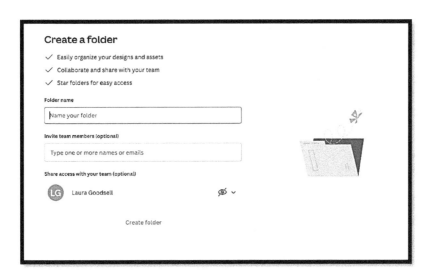

Don't worry about the second choice if you're not going to make a team. We'll only set up a simple folder for this exercise.
4.   Click the button that says "**Create Folder**" at the very bottom.
5.   Your folder will now be added to the page's **Folders** area. If you click on a folder or the three dots next to it, you can change how it looks.

You can also click on the star icon next to the name of your new folder to make it the main folder. It's going to turn yellow. It will now appear in the menu bar on the left. You can make as many files as you want, and it works great for everyone. You can make folders inside of files up to five levels deep to save even more space. Lastly, you can share a folder with someone on your team from the Folders menu. They must already have a Canva account, though, because you can't share a folder with someone who isn't on your team. We have already talked about what Canva is, how to use it, how to set up our account on both a computer and a phone, and how the two main Canva accounts are different. Our thoughts are better organized now that we're working on them in groups. Next, let's look at the Content Planner.

Arranging Content with the Content Planner

This app from Canva is great for people who use social media and plan posts. You can make posts in Canva and plan them to go out on different social networks at different times. This means you don't need to sign up for extra sites and apps to add your content. It's on the right side of the main page. You won't be able to use this feature if you are on Free, though. It's possible to get a free trial for 30 days and see if you like it enough to use it again. The Content Planner is set up like a calendar, so you can change months at the top. You can see where and when you're planning to post at a look. It also shows major holidays and world events. If you need to make something for an event, all you have to do is click on the event name, and it will bring up a list of templates that have already been made for that date:

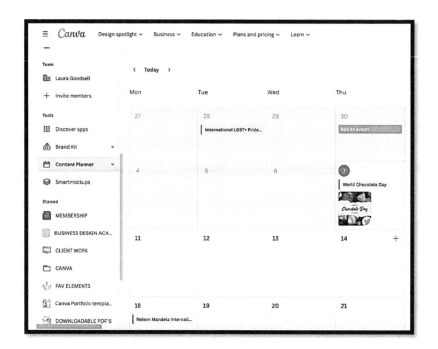

This link took me to the page for **International Yoga Day**. After that, I can click on the following to begin writing my post about International Yoga Day:

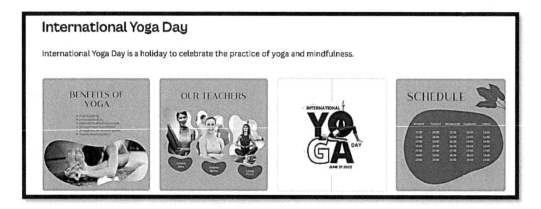

Creating and Scheduling a Post

You can do this in a few different ways with Canva, so I'll show you step-by-step how to schedule content for your social media links. You only need to make a picture and pick a date on the calendar to make a post. When I clicked on the date I wanted to use, my designs showed up at the top. At the bottom, there was a list of ready-made templates. In the middle to the right, you could also choose to start over. This time, I'll use a template that's already been made:

Once I choose a template, it will open in the normal view for changing templates. I can now change the words, pictures, and colors to make it fit my brand.

Once you are done making changes to your template, you can set a time. Click the **Share** button in the top right corner:

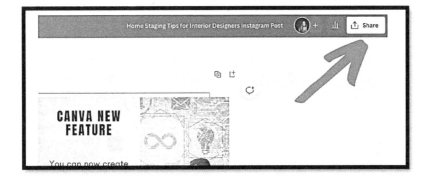

There'll be a drop-down menu. You might have to click "**More**" at the bottom to find the **Schedule** button.

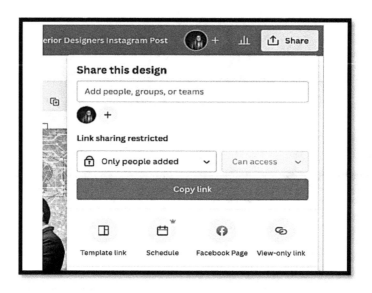

Once you click the "**More**" button, you'll see all of your choices, such as the Schedule tab and all the social media sites you can post straight to. This is where you will find all of your choices in Canva. When you see "**Schedule**," scroll down and click on it. It will be in the **Social** area. After that, it will show you boxes where you can write your post, pick your channel, and change the date and time you want it to go live. When you click on the date, a calendar will appear. Once you've picked out the date, you can pick the time. Then you can pick which channel to watch. Now you need to connect your social accounts to Canva. The one with Facebook is the only one that isn't easy. You'll need to sign in to Facebook and let Canva log in as you. You can also connect to post straight to Instagram, which is the most popular site. There is, however, one thing that you can't do: join a Creator account. Most of the time, though, they only need your Canva login information. It can link itself if you are already logged in on another computer. The "**Select a channel**" link at the bottom of the list will let you do this. It will show up at the top after you join, and you can pick which channel you want to use:

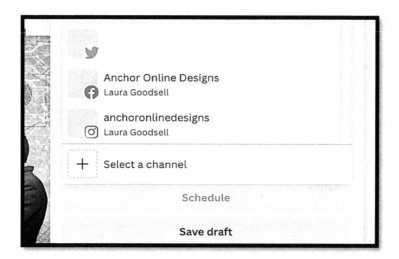

In the end, you need to write your message like you would on a social media site. You can even stick to the number of characters you have with Canva. At the very bottom right, it will show you how many words you've used on each page. Twitter lets you use 280 characters; while Facebook lets you use 5,000 characters. You can now click **Schedule** or save your post as a draft to work on it later. You can find these options right on the Content Planner calendar. After making the design, click the "**Make a copy**" button to send the same post to a different site. You can only use this button once on each station.

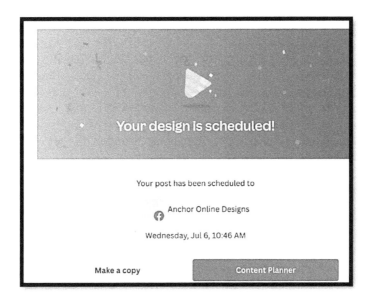

We are going to look at our post in the Content Planner. I can now see all the posts I had planned. It will tell you the time and place where it will go if you move your mouse over one. You can plan more than one post for different places on the same day. It will show a smaller icon for each platform so you can quickly see where everything is set to upload:

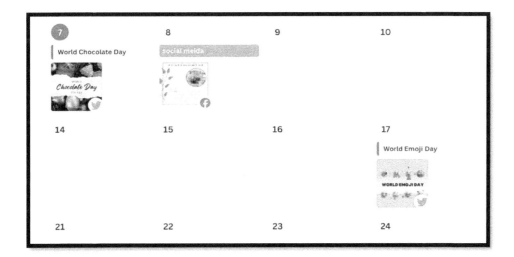

If you need to, you can change any post you have planned. When you click on the post in Content Planner, the planned post will appear, and you can make changes to it. Just click **Save and Schedule** when you're done.

Other Ways to Schedule and Post

I thought it would be helpful to quickly go over the other ways you can use Canva to plan and post to social media sites that do the same thing and are pretty much the same process. **You can do these two things with Canva on both phones and computers:**

- The first step is to make a plan, but don't pick a date in the Content Planner yet. Start a new template and make your drawing. Then, go to the menu and choose "**Schedule.**"
- Second, you don't need to plan anything; you can post on any site right away. Just click "**Share**" and pick your platform from the list that appears. Another screen will appear, but this one has a "**Publish now**" button instead of the "Arrange" button. After getting your pictures, you don't have to save them to your phone or computer and then share them on social media. If you click on the small calendar button in the bottom left corner, you can still use this drop-down to make plans for:

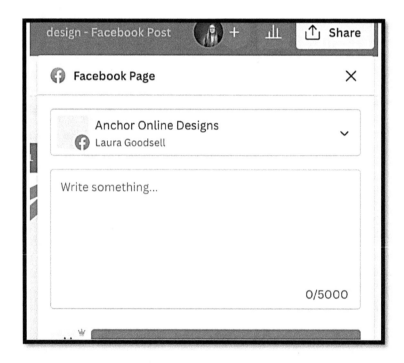

You can save a lot of time by planning and writing a lot of posts at once. This will help you decide what to write each day. The Content Planner is a great tool for your business that can help you. It's also free because it's part of Pro.

CHAPTER 4
CANVA MOBILE APP
The Basic Features of the Canva App

The app's main area is made up of four screens: Home, Projects, Templates, and Canva Pro. Allow us to go over each part and what it holds.

The Home Screen

We'll start with **Home**, which is the first thing you see when you log in and open the app. It looks like most social apps, so it's pretty simple to use. At the top of the screen is the **menu button**. It lets you do some of the same things as the tabs, like **Projects and Templates**. As a Pro member, you can only get **Content Planner and Brand Hub**. However, you can also connect more advanced tools and apps with Canva, like **Smartmokups.** There is a **search bar** next to the choices. Keywords can help you find projects or templates that you have already finished. Below that, there are tabs that let you see the thousands of templates that come with the software. "**For You**" will be different each time you open the app, like how Spotify does, based on how you use Canva. Most of the time, it will show you your most recent projects, different design sizes, and templates that you might be interested in. Each one will be clearly labeled with what it's for. You can start working on different kinds of templates in other tabs, like ones for **social media, videos, presentations, prints,** and more. The page will change to show you everything you can do about that subject if you click on any of them.

From the home screen, you can start making a new picture in a number of ways. When you click on a template you like, a new window will appear where you can begin making changes. To make a design, click on the type of design you want, such as Post or Video for Instagram. You can pick a template or start from scratch on this page. Also, press the **purple plus (+)** sign at the bottom of the screen to start over. You can choose the size (Custom or something like Facebook Post) when you tap it. After that, a new, empty space will appear.

The Projects Screen

You can see all the things you've made on your computer, phone, or account on the Projects screen. You can see the files, photos, and thoughts you store in the cloud. In the upper right part of each drawing picture are two buttons. The arrow icon lets you download the picture and the three dots icon brings up a menu with many options, such as **Edit, Make a Copy,** and **Share**.

Remember that **Edit** will change the picture you had before. Instead, click "**Make a Copy**" if you like your design and want to keep it for later use.

The Templates Screen

It's kind of like the home screen, but this one is mostly about templates. You can look through each template or by subject with the buttons at the top. You can also look at what other Canva users have picked as a theme, such as Earth Day or Juneteenth. Holidays or times of the year are often to blame. You can find areas like **Features Collections, Trending Near You, New on Canva**, and more. All of them are meant to give you ideas.

The Canva Pro Screen

You can see the last shot if you pay for the service. This is where you'll find options like **Brand Kit, Premium Content,** and social media plans.

Create and Modify Your Design

Now let's talk about the picture-making tools you can use. To start, choose one of the templates. We used an Instagram post. Keep in mind that not all templates can be used with a free account. Try to find templates that don't say "Pro" or "Paid." This picture lets you change any part of it by clicking on the words, pictures, background, or shapes. You can also move it around, and the app will help you line up things in the middle or with other things in the shot. The **Undo** and **Redo** buttons are in the upper left corner. They look like two round lines pointing in different directions. If you don't like any of the changes you made, click them. When you tap on a different part of the screen, you get a different set of choices. They can be found in the bar at the bottom of the screen. There is a "**Replace**" button on this picture. If you press it, you can add a picture from your phone's gallery, take a picture with your camera, or pick one by Canva.

On top of that, you can crop the picture; add colors and effects make it move, and more. To change something, tap a text box once and then press **Edit**. After that, you can change the style, size, layout, and other things. The **Nudge** tool makes a big difference. With the direction buttons, you can move things by just one pixel at a time. This is better for precision than a touch screen. You can also add new things to the design by pressing the plus (+) button. You can change the template (which will replace the current template), add sound and pictures, change the background, and get to all of your files from that page.

Download or Share Your Canva Design

It's time to use the picture (or movie) that you've changed everything about to make it perfect. To do that, press the buttons at the top of the screen. The down arrow saves the picture to your phone, and the up arrow lets you share it with other people. The Share button is great about the Canva app. When you're done with your picture, you can use WhatsApp or Slack to send it straight to work or friends. If you press the "**Share**" button, you can also post your picture straight to Instagram or TikTok. If you were on a PC, you would have to first move the picture to your phone. You can even set the post to go live on social media at a certain time if you have a Pro account.

Working with Grids and Frames

Grids in Canva

When you use grids in Canva, creating can be fun and easy. Grids help put colors, videos, pictures, and even text into neat groups. They make any design look finished and professional. Grids offer an easy structure to make designs stand out, whether you're making a mood board, a photo collage, or a marketing flyer. Canva has a lot of grid choices that can be accessed directly from their platform for people who want to start. Users can pick between single-frame grids for simple designs and multi-frame grids that let them mix and match different features. Because of this, even people who are just starting out can make designs that look great. Grids aren't just boxes; they can be used to tell stories. Designers can frame portions of a picture with grids, add color, or even arrange elements to draw viewers' attention to certain areas. By looking into the different ways grids can be used, you can easily turn a simple design into a striking one.

Navigating to Grid Tools in Canva

Grids in Canva help create neat and professional designs. They offer a way to arrange multiple images or features in a simple format. Users find grids easy to work with, whether they're on a computer or a mobile device. To start, open a new or current design in Canva. Look at the left side of the Canva editor. You'll see choices like Photos, Text, and Elements. Pick out **Elements**. In the search bar, look for "grids" once you're inside. This shows a list of single-frame and multi-frame grids. People can choose the type that works best for their design. You could also just type "grids" into the main search bar. With this feature, you can quickly find grid tools without having to scroll through the sections. When people click on a grid, it adds to their design right away. After that, they can change the grid's size and position to fit their painting. You can just drag pictures or movies into the grid. This action cuts and fits them perfectly on its own. If you have any problems while using grids, the Canva Help Center has more information on how to do it. You can find video lessons on YouTube that can help you learn by showing you how to do something.

Selecting the Right Grid for Your Design

It can really help your design work if you pick the right grid in Canva. There are different grid patterns and choices between custom and pre-set grids. Finding the right one for your project will make it look better.

Grid Varieties and Layouts

Grids come in many shapes and sizes. Single-image grids, multiple-photo layouts, and collage grids are all common design elements. Each type is used for a different thing. Single-image grids are great for drawing attention to a single picture. Multi-photo setups are the best way to show off a group of photos or tell a story. Grids can also be of different sizes and shapes. There are grids that are square, oblong, and even round. When it comes to social media posts, circular grids give them a unique look. The content you want to draw attention to and the general look will help you choose the right shape.

Custom Grids vs. Pre-Set Grids

The artists in Canva can pick between custom grids and grids that are already set up. **Custom grids** give you the freedom to make them fit your needs. Users can change the grid's sizes and empty areas to suit their needs. This works great for people who know exactly how they want their plan to look. **Pre-set grids** make designing easier by giving you choices that are already made. For beginners or people who don't have much time, they're great. Pre-set grids help make sure that the makeup is balanced without having to make many changes. Think about the project needs and skill level when deciding between the two. Canva gives you the tools to make great designs, whether you choose a custom grid or a plan that's already been made.

Adding Grids to Your Canvas

Adding grids to your Canva design can help you arrange elements in a way that looks good. Grids make it simple to organize text, images, and other elements, which speeds up the design process and increases the interest in finished projects.

Dragging and Dropping Grid Elements

You can use grids right away by dragging and dropping them on your painting. If you want to find grids in Canva, type "grids" into the search bar. Pick out the grid you want to use, then click and drag it to your painting. The grid, which can hold pictures, movies, or color blocks, is put in place by this action.

Adjusting Grid Sizes

It's easy to change the size of the grids once they are on the painting. When you click on the grid, handles appear on the sides that you can drag to change the size of the grid. By resizing, the designer can make sure that the grid fits exactly into the layout they want, making sure it goes with the rest of the project.

Resizing and Aligning Content

In Canva, you can change the size of grids to make the design fit the needs of your project. The "Resize" handle on the grid makes it easy for users to change its size. This feature lets the designer change the size of the grid to fit the layout they want, making sure that the text and images inside each grid area are easy to see and the right size.

Filling Grids with Images

With Canva's grids, you can arrange pictures in a lot of different ways. People can add pictures to a grid by clicking on the spot in the grid where they want to put the picture. They can choose Photos from the side panel to look through the pictures that are there. They can also click **Uploads** and post their own instead. If you drag and drop an image onto a grid spot, it will be resized to fit instantly. One more benefit is that you can quickly switch between pictures by dragging a new one over the old one. This gives you options without having to start from scratch.

Overlaying Text on Grids

It's easy to add information or style to designs by putting text on top of grids. Once the grid is chosen, users can click **Text** on the side panel to pick from different text styles. They can type right on the grid and change the color, size, and style. Positioning is very important, so move the text box around to fit the design. This could mean changing it to a less busy part of the picture so it's easier to read. Text can stand out better against different backgrounds with the help of shadows and borders.

Layering Multiple Grids

Putting grids on top of each other helps you make designs with lots of different parts. By stacking grids on top of each other, designers can quickly arrange content into rows and columns, letting each section highlight different parts. By putting images, text, and graphics on top of each other, this method gives you more design choices. Pick out the base grid to begin layering grids. Pick a grid with the right number of frames to add on top of the first one. Change the size and position so that it fits in the base grid. This method makes sure the layout is clean and organized, which is great for presentations or images with more than one subject.

Frames in Canva

Frames are an important part of Canva for making designs that are bright and lively. They give users placeholders that let them place pictures in creative ways within a shaped area, which makes any project look better.

The Basic Concepts of Frames

In Canva, frames are like empty boxes that can hold pictures or photos. These frames make it easy for people to put their photos in a variety of shapes and layouts. When someone drags a picture over a frame, the picture changes shape to fit the frame. With this feature, you can make quick changes without having to use complicated editing tools. Users can easily switch out the pictures inside the frames, which makes it a useful choice for any design job. It works for people of all skill levels, making design easy to do and fun.

Different Types of Frames Available

Canva has many frames, and each one is good for a different kind of design. To get to the frames area, users should go to the Elements tab and scroll down until they find it. They can pick from circles, rectangles, letters, and even shapes that aren't real shapes.

Adding Frames to Your Design

Frames in Canva let user's crop pictures into shapes that make designs look better. Users can use this part to learn how to find frames, place them, and change their sizes in their design projects.

Using the Search Bar to Find Frames

To find frames in Canva, users should first open their design project. They should click on the "**Elements**" tab on the editor's side tray. They can use the search bar and type in "frame." This will bring up a list of frames from which they can choose. The frames come in many styles and shapes, so there are many choices to meet the needs of any design.

Placing Frames onto the Canvas

When you choose a frame, you can click on it to add it straight to the canvas. People can drag and drop the frame to where they want it to go. You should be careful about where you put the frame so that it fits well with other design elements. The frame will be used to hold pictures. Users can click and drag pictures into the frame from their own uploads or from Canva's library. This makes it so that the picture fits perfectly into the frame shape you choose, giving it a finished look.

Resizing and Repositioning Frames

Once a frame is in place, it's easy to change its size. When someone clicks on the frame, they can use the corner buttons to change its size. By holding down the **Shift** key while adjusting, the frame's proportions are kept. Clicking and dragging the frame to a different spot on the image is one way to move it. For accurate placing, Canva has grid lines and snap-to-grid tools.

Customizing Frames

By changing the frames in Canva, users can make designs that are truly unique and their own. You can make your projects stand out and show off your own style by changing colors, adding effects, and putting frames on top of other elements.

Changing Frame Colors

Changing the color of frames can make a big difference in how they look and help them fit in with the theme of your design. Some frames have colors that are already set, but others let people change these. To change the color of a frame, click on it and find the "color palette" button. This feature can be seen if the frame lets you change the colors. Next, pick the colors you want to use that go with your general design theme.

Adding Effects to Frames

When you add effects to frames, they get extra details and look better, which makes each design more interesting. Some effects that give things depth are shadows, glows, and outlines. Click on the frame and go to the effects panel to add effects. Users can try out different choices here, such as the brightness of the glow or the strength of the shadow. These effects shouldn't take away from the design, but they should also not be too strong.

Layering Frames with Other Elements

Adding frames to other design elements, like text, shapes, or pictures, is called layering. This method makes an arrangement that is rich and interesting to look at. First, pick out the frame and move it over the parts of your painting that you want to include. It's important to use the arrange tool to choose which part should go on top or below. In order to set the right visual ordering, this will help.

Working with Images and Frames

Canva's frames make it easy to add and change pictures to make any design better. It's easy for users to add photos, change how they fit, and switch them out. To begin working with pictures and frames, follow these steps.

Inserting Images into Frames

First, users should go to the Canva parts library and pick out the frame they want. They can either use the **Uploads** tab to add their own pictures or the **Photos** area of the Canva editor to look for pictures. If you pick an image and then drag it over the frame you want, it will automatically snap into place. This quick and easy method saves time and makes sure the picture fits the frame without having to be adjusted by hand.

Adjusting Images within Frames

After putting a picture in a frame, users can change it to make it look just right for their design. They can zoom in or out and move the picture around in Canva to bring out certain details. They can get to these choices by clicking on the frame, which will bring up a toolbar. With the zoom tool, they can zoom in on important parts of the picture or get rid of unwanted parts. Users may also want to click and drag the picture to move it around in the frame. By doing this, they can make an arrangement that is balanced and looks good.

Replacing Images in Frames

It's easy and quick to switch out a picture for another. Dragging a new photo over an old one is all it takes to change the picture in a frame. When this action is taken, the picture will be replaced automatically, without the user having to first delete it.

Creating Custom Frame Layouts

Frames make it easy to change how plans look. Users can change the size, position, and style of frames to suit their design needs. Canva has a lot of different frame styles, from simple edges to more unique shapes. The size and color of the frames can be easily changed to fit the style of the project. Custom frame layouts can help you arrange text, pictures, and other things on a page so it looks clean and professional.

CHAPTER 5

TEXT AND TYPOGRAPHY

Adding and Editing Text

Adding text to Canva is a great way to get used to how it works and how the design tools are set up. In design, the writing tool is on the left side of the screen.

Step 1: Accessing the Text Tool

Start with a blank canvas or open your design project to add words. There is a toolbar with different choices on the left side of Canva's interface. Click on the **Text** tab when you find it. **This will bring up a window with three simple text options:**
1. **Add a Heading**: For large, attention-grabbing text, such as titles or main headers.
2. **Add a Subheading**: Slightly smaller text, suitable for secondary titles or supporting content.
3. **Add a Body Text**: For longer pieces of text, such as paragraphs or detailed information.

If you click on one of these choices, you can pick it, or you can click and drag the text type right onto your canvas.

Step 2: Adding Text from Scratch

Simply click on the canvas and press the "**T**" key on your computer to make a text box by hand. This shortcut adds a new text box in the middle of the image without you having to do anything. The default text will show up, and you can type your own content straight to replace it.

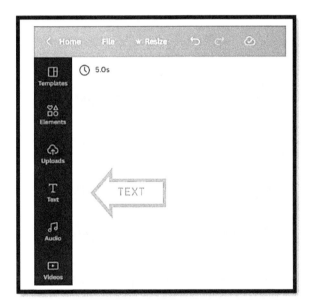

Editing Text in Canva

Double-click the text box that you want to edit.
1. Delete or edit its contents. Use the text edit options on the editor toolbar to format your text.
2. Click outside the text box to finish.

Choosing Font

1. Click the **font dropdown** from the toolbar.
2. Find the font you want to use or pick it out.

Note: If you have a Canva Pro account, you can access an extra 5,000 fonts. This makes it easy to find fonts that no one else is using.

Text Size

Click on the font size you want to change and type in the new size. You can also click on the plus or minus signs to make the area bigger or smaller.

Text Color

Click **Text Color** and select a new color from the color panel.

Text Emphasis

Click **Bold**, **Italics**, or **Underline** to add emphasis to text. If these icons are grayed out, it means that the current font used doesn't support adding emphasis.

Text Alignment

Repeatedly click on **Center, Left, Right,** or **Justify** until the layout you want is used.

List

1. To make your text into a bullet list, click **Bullet List.**
2. To put your text in a list with numbers, click on the **Bullet list** icon again. This will change the bullets to numbers.

Text Spacing

1. Press **Text spacing.**
2. Move the **letter spacing** and **line spacing** sliders to the number you want.

Font Pairing

Let's say your brand has a sharp look, a bright color scheme, and messages that are easy to understand. Think of Comic Sans and Papyrus all over it. Yes? That's the magic (or lack of magic) of putting fonts together. Like a friendly guide, they whisper your personality, make your writing easier to read, and help people find their way through your stuff as the voice of your brand. You might see a clean headline with serifs that grab your attention, then soft text that doesn't have any serifs. You can talk to it and see it in a way that makes the important parts stand out without making your eyes melt. Take a look at the same message written in Comic Sans with all capital letters. It would look like a mess. Friends, fonts are what make a brand "wow" or "whoa, back up!" Let's stop fighting about style and use the power of pairs of fonts instead!

Understanding Font Pairing Principles

Putting fonts together that look good is a big part of graphic design. To do this, you need to know the basic rules of font matching, such as how to balance, contrast, and line fonts. **This is how these ideas can be broken down:**

- **Contrast:** Contrast is an important part of font pairing because it makes your design look interesting and balanced. If you mix fonts with different styles, like sans-serif and serif fonts, font or bold show font, and normal fonts, you can get a lot of different looks.
- **Balance:** It's also important to make sure that the parts of your design are spread out properly and look good. Another important rule for the best pairs of Canva fonts is this one. Think about the fonts' size, weight, and scale, and make the changes that are needed to make them look good together.
- **Compatibility:** This refers to how well the styles you're pairing read and look with each other. You need to think about both the overall message and tone of your design as well as the specific styles you're using to make sure everything fits together.

You can pair fonts in ways that look good, make the design better, and make it easier to read if you know and follow these rules. Don't be afraid to break the "rules" when you find a good pair of fonts. As you get better, you'll get really good at putting fonts together in ways that look great.

The Best Creative Canva Font Pairings

Lovelo & Gistesy

Lovelo is a modern, strong style that makes you feel good about yourself. This method works really well for titles and headlines. It looks very different when paired with Gistesy, a sleek and beautiful script font. Strong lines from Lovelo and smooth curves from Gistesy work well together to make designs more interesting and classier. This mix could be used to make graphics for social media or brand products that stand out.

Le Jour Serif & Hero Light

The sans serif font Le Jour Serif looks good for a long time. Because it has clean lines and can be used in many ways, it looks good in a lot of different design styles. Hero Light is a simple sans-serif font that looks great with it for a modern and stylish look. Hero Light is a simple font that looks good with the classic style of Le Jour Serif. Both of them work well together for news stories or blogs.

Quiche Bold & Poppins

Quiche Bold
Poppins

Quiche Bold is a great pattern to choose if you want something modern and stylish. It can be used for big headlines and messages because it has strong geometric shapes. Quiche Bold makes its effect stand out even more when it is used with Poppins, a flexible sans-serif font. This mix makes your designs look professional and is simple to read, so it's great for brochures, slideshows, or product boxes.

Versailles & Open sans Light

VERSAILLES
Open Sans Light

You can look classy and polished if you wear Versailles with Open Sans Light. The fancy letter style Versailles makes you feel rich and well-off. This makes a nice contrast with Open Sans Light's clean and light style, making it both interesting to look at and easy to read. That mix works great for high-end business cards, wedding invitations, and event signs.

Lemon Tuesday & Aileron Thin

Lemon Tuesday
Aileron Thin

Lemon Tuesday is another great choice. It has a fun and lively vibe that you can use in your designs. It's so cute that it looks like it was made by hand. Aileron Thin is a light and thin sans-serif font that looks good with Lemon Tuesday because it brings out the color of the text. This pair looks great together in kids' books, on this fun social media post, or in creative branding materials.

Implementing Canva Font Pairings

Now that you know about these lovely Canva font pairs, it's time to use them in your work. Here are some tips to get the most out of these sets:

1. **Maintain visual harmony**: To keep the design looking good, make sure that the font pairs you choose match the overall mood and theme of the design.
2. **Consider hierarchy**: Use different font sizes, weights, and styles to make a clear visual order. The reader will be able to see what they need to see well.
3. **Experiment and iterate**: Try new things and keep trying them. Don't be afraid to mix and match fonts and styles. You can try out different combinations to find the best one for your design.
4. **Stay consistent**: Once you decide on a font pair, use it throughout your design to make it look unified and professional.

By using these sets of fonts, you can take your creativity and design skills to a whole new level in Canva.

Exploring Additional Font Pairings

Not only the pairs that were already stated, but Canva has a huge number of fonts that you can try out. Think of more than a few different pairs. Check out other pairs that match your style and project needs. The combinations you find might surprise you and work well with your design goals.

Text Effects and Styles

Applying Text Effects

Text can be given effects in a number of different ways on Canva. You can add effects to text using the Text tool or the Text Format options in the Format menu. To see the text effects, select the text you want to change and click "**Effects**" in the tool bar. On the left, you'll see two groups: style effects and shape effects. First, we'll check out the style effects. Let's have fun with these cool word effects. As we go through the styles, we'll talk about what they do.

Shadow

It makes your words look like they have a shadow. There are some things you can do to change how the shadow looks. The knobs can be moved to the left or right to get each setting just right. The options shown are what they should be. You can change offset to change how far away the shade is from the words. From the words, the direction can change the line of the shadow. For each shade, blur and transparency can be used to change how see-through the shadow is. By clicking on the color tile below and selecting the desired color from the left-hand design box, we can also change the color of the shadow.

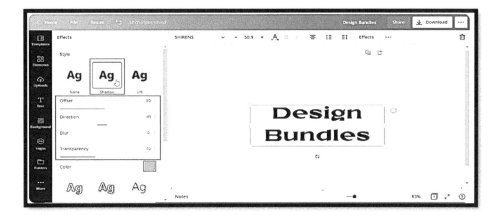

Lift

It looks like your writing is being pulled off the page with this effect. You can only change how strong the shadow is behind the words with this effect. You can make the fuzzy shade stronger by moving the tool to the right. You can make it weaker by moving it to the left.

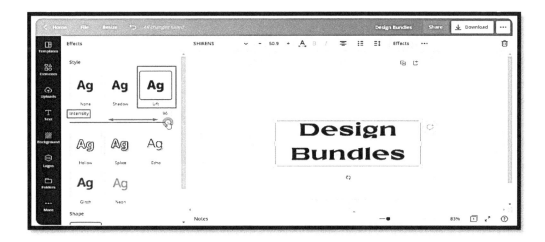

Hollow

The letters get smoothed out with this effect, making your text stand out. It works best with styles that are thick, not thin. The width tool lets you change how thick your shape is.

The hollow effect can also be used to make the edges of your text smooth. To make one, you should start with a good text. On the toolbar, click the three dots to show more choices. Then, press the copy button to make a copy of your text. To change the contrast of your original text, click on the color tile and pick a color from the list on the left.

Pick the second word; it should be black. Then, go to **Effects** and click on **Hollow** in the list on the left. Put the outline text on top of the heavy text.

Splice

The next effect, Splice, is a mix of the empty effect and the shadow effect. You can move the control bar four times to make your split text look different. You can change how **thick** the text outline is, how far the shadow goes away from the text outline, and the **direction** of the shadow text behind the outline text. You can also change the color of the shadow text by clicking on the color tile below and choosing the color you want from the editor panel on the left.

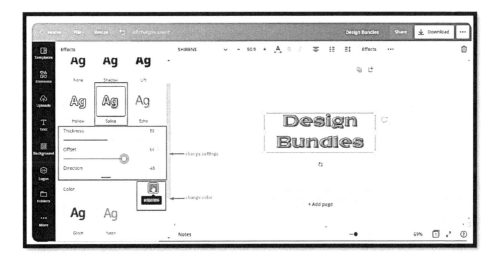

Echo

Echo copies your text twice and puts them behind each other to make it look like it's stacked. You can change things by offset, direction, and color. Offset changes how far away the main text is from the shadow text. The shadow text moves behind the main text in different directions. And the color changes the shadow text's color. You can see it better when the font isn't too thick or too small.

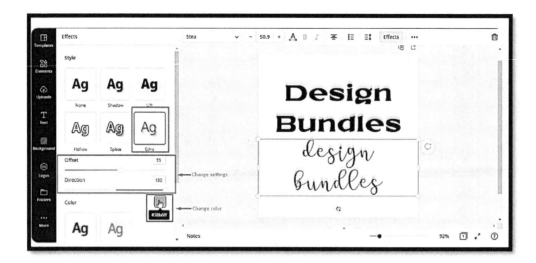

Glitch

An effect called "glitch" will make your text look like it's not lined up straight. You can change things by offset, direction, and color. Gap changes how much of a gap there is, and Color changes what color the glitch is. You can only glitch in electric cyan, light neon pink, neon blue, and bright red. It looks good on both thick and thin letters with the glitch effect.

Neon

Your text looks like it's from the 1980s because of the neon effect's bright glow. You can only change how bright the neon glow is with this effect. The glow gets stronger when you move the tool to the left, but the word gets less clear. By moving it to the right, the writing is clear and the glow is less strong.

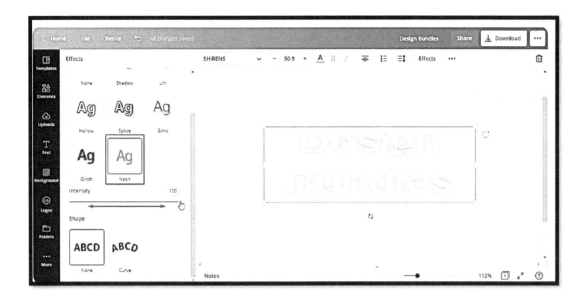

Curve

We're done with all the style effects. The only shape effect is curve text, which is what we'll talk about next. You can curve text with Curve. If you move the curve tool to the right, you can change how strong the curve is. It lets you turn your words into either a half-circle or a full-circle.

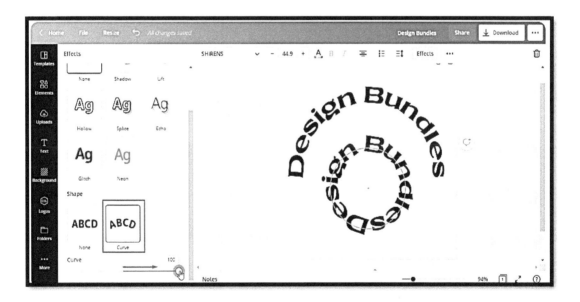

You can change the curve's angle in a different way if you move the curve tool to the left.

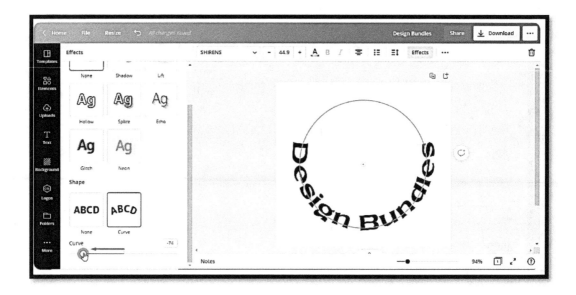

One last thing to remember about Canva text effects is that any of them can make your text stand out, but you should only use a few of them in your design. Also, remember that they only look good on title texts, not body texts.

TIP: You might not be able to read the text after adding effects to it in Canva.

Text Alignment Options

TIP: In Canva, it's easy to line things up wrong if you're not careful. If something isn't lined up right, you can always use the alignment tools to fix it. But if you don't know how to use the positioning tools, you might make a bad plan. The first way you can align text is by using the **text alignment buttons** in the toolbar. Choose the words you want to match and click on one of the "Align" buttons. You can choose to left-align, center-align, right-align, or justify.

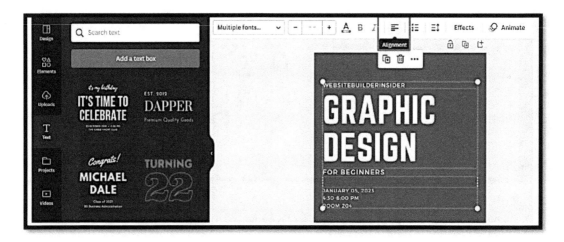

There is another way to fix text. Use the choices in the Text Properties menu. Click on the "**T**" button in the toolbar or double-click on the word you want to align. This will bring up the menu. Then, in the **Text Properties** menu, click on "**Alignment**" and select the alignment method you want from the drop-down menu that appears. The third way to align text is to use the alignment choices in the **Format Menu**. To get to this page, click on the "**Format**" tab at the top of the Canva Designer. Next, find "**Text alignment**" in the Format Menu. Click on the drop-down menu next to it and pick the type of alignment you want.

Finally, you can align text in HTML code in a fourth way. To do this, add the value "**align=left**", "**align=center**", "**align=right**", or "**align=justify**" to the beginning tag of your text. That's all there is to it! There are four different ways to arrange text in Canva. Get in touch with our support team or look at our Help Center if you need more help with how to use Canva.

CHAPTER 6

WORKING WITH IMAGES AND GRAPHICS

Uploading Your Own Images

1. **Log in to Your Canva Account**: Go to www.canva.com and sign in to your Canva account. Choose or create a design project once you're logged in.
2. **Locate the Uploads Tab**: The **Uploads** tab is on the left side of the design editor's toolbar. This section is where you can manage the pictures, videos, and audio clips you share.
3. **Click the "Upload Files" Button**: Click the "**Upload Files**" button. This can be found in the Uploads tab. You can look through your computer for the picture(s) you want to share in a file explorer window that will pop up.
4. **Select Your Image(s)**: Pick one or more pictures from your phone or tablet and press **Open** (or something similar, based on your OS). Canva works with many picture file types, such as JPEG, PNG, and SVG.
5. **Wait for Upload Completion**: The pictures you uploaded will show up in the Uploads tab. While the file is being uploaded, a progress bar will appear. Once the process is finished, you will be able to view the image.
6. **Drag and Drop onto the Canvas**: Once the picture is uploaded, you can drag it from the Uploads panel straight onto your painting. You can change the image's size, position, and other settings as needed.

Uploading Images on Canva's Mobile App

1. **Open the Canva App**: Launch the Canva app on your smartphone or tablet and sign in to your account.
2. **Access the Uploads Section**: Open your design project and tap the **+** button at the bottom of the screen. From the options that appear, select **Uploads**.
3. **Upload Files from Your Device**: Tap the **Upload Media** button and choose images from your device's gallery, file manager, or cloud storage.
4. **Insert Images into Your Design**: Once uploaded, the image will be stored in the Uploads section. Tap the image to insert it into your canvas and customize it as needed.

Customizing Uploaded Images

Once you've uploaded your pictures, Canva gives you a lot of tools to improve them and add them to your design.

Resizing and Positioning

- **Resize**: To change the size of the picture, use the handles on its corners. You can drag the picture in or out to make it bigger or smaller.

- **Reposition**: To move the picture around the board, click and drag it. It will show up with alignment guides to help you put it in the right place.

Cropping

- **Crop Tool**: Either double-click the picture or go to the toolbar and choose "crop." You can focus on the part of the picture you want by moving the cropping handles.

Filters and Adjustments

- To change the mood of your picture, use one of Canva's pre-designed filters, or directly change brightness, contrast, and saturation.
- Experiment with effects like vignettes or tints to create a professional or artistic look.

Transparency

- Use the transparency slider to adjust the opacity of your picture. This can be used to make backgrounds that aren't too noticeable or to put images on top of other parts.

Frames and Shapes

From the Elements tab, drag the picture you just uploaded into a frame or shape to make it fit into certain layouts or make your own cutouts.

Background Removal (Canva Pro Feature)

The background remover tool in Canva Pro lets you focus on the subject of your picture by getting rid of the background with just one click. This function is great for making pictures of products or profile pictures.

Managing Uploaded Images

The Uploads tab in Canva organizes the pictures you upload, making it easy to find them and use them in different tasks. Here are some ways to keep track of your files:
- **File Organization**: Delete uploads that you don't need to keep your library clean and easy to use.
- **Reuse Images**: Once you share an image, it stays in your account and can be used in other designs without having to be uploaded again.
- **Folders (Canva Pro Feature)**: Put your shared photos in folders to make them easy to find. This is especially useful for companies or groups that are in charge of a lot of assets.

Tips for Optimizing Uploaded Images

1. **Choose High-Quality Images**: Upload images with high quality to make sure they look clear and professional, especially for printed designs.
2. **Compress Large Files**: To avoid uploading files slowly, reduce the size of big-picture files without losing quality. Some tools, like TinyPNG, can help you shrink files before you share them.
3. **Use Transparent Backgrounds (PNG)**: If you need a picture with no background, like a logo or icon, use a PNG file with a transparent background.
4. **Respect Copyrights**: Before you share any pictures, make sure you have the legal right to do so. Do not use information that is protected by copyright unless you own it or have permission from the owner of the copyright.

Common Issues and Troubleshooting

1. **Slow Uploads**: If you're having trouble uploading, check your internet link. Cutting down on the file size can also help.
2. **Unsupported File Types**: Generally, Canva works with image files like JPEG, PNG, and SVG. Make sure your file is in one of these types if it won't upload.
3. **Image Distortion**: If an image looks like it's made up of pixels, it may not have enough sharpness for the size you want to use it in. Change it to a file with a better resolution.

Using Canva's Photo Library

The photo library in Canva is a huge collection of high-quality pictures that you can use to make your designs better. This feature gives users access to millions of photos that can be used for almost any purpose, from personal projects to business branding, marketing campaigns, and educational materials. It's easy to find, choose, and change photos that fit your creative idea because the photo library is built into Canva's interface. If you know how to use Canva's picture library well, you can make your designs look better and save time because you won't have to look for images on other sites.

Accessing Canva's Photo Library

As you work in Canva's design editor, the picture library is usually under the **Photos** tab on the left-hand toolbar. This area is where you can find a carefully chosen collection of stock photos that are organized by style, subject, and theme. The library has a lot of different kinds of pictures to meet your needs, whether you're looking for pictures of scenery, people, food, abstract patterns, or business-related pictures. Just click on the **Photos** tab to get to the library. You can look through popular groups, search by keyword, or use filters to narrow down your search from here. There are both free and paid images in Canva's picture library. Paid images are indicated by a crown icon. You can get access to premium pictures with a Canva Pro subscription or pay a small fee for each one.

Finding the Right Photo

Search Functionality

The search bar in the Photos tab is one of the best ways to quickly find the right picture. Type in words that describe what you want, like "mountains," "office desk," or "summer vibes." Canva's smart search algorithm will then show you results that match your query, often with ideas to help you narrow down your choices. If you're making a graphic for a travel blog and looking for "beach," the library might also suggest "sunset beach," "tropical beach," or "beach activities." This is a great feature to have when you're not sure what style of graphics you want.

Exploring Categories

Canva sorts its photo library into groups, which makes it easy to find pictures that fit the theme of your project. Some of the most common categories are nature, technology, business, education, fashion, and way of life. Looking through these groups is a great way to get ideas or find pictures that fit the mood and purpose of your design.

Filtering Options

Canva has screening tools that let you narrow down your search results by:
- **Color**: Choose a color filter to match images to the color scheme of your design.
- **Orientation**: Based on the plan of your design, you can choose between landscape, portrait, or square orientations.
- **Image Type**: Depending on what you need, you can filter the results to only show pictures or drawings.

Using filters will help you quickly find the most relevant pictures without having to look through content that isn't related.

Adding Photos to Your Design

When you choose a picture from Canva's library, all you have to do to add it to your design is click or drag it onto the canvas. The photo will instantly fit the layout, but you can change where it appears, how big it is, and how it fits into your design even more.

Positioning

Once you've put the picture where you want it, click and drag it to move it around the board. The alignment guides in Canva will show up to help you center or line up the photo with other parts of your design.

Resizing

You can change the size of the picture by dragging its sides. Canva makes sure that the aspect ratio stays the same unless you crop or distort the picture on purpose.

Cropping

Use Canva's crop tool if the picture needs to fit into a certain frame or has parts that aren't needed. To change the area that can be seen, double-click the picture or use the crop tool in the toolbar.

Using Frames and Grids

The frames and grids in Canva are great for adding photos to well-organized layouts. If you drag a picture into a frame or grid, it will stay there by itself. This is especially helpful for making collages, mood boards, or designs with more than one picture.

Customizing Photos

The photo library on Canva does more than just have pictures; it also has tools to change and improve them so they fit the style of your project. With these tools, you can take a stock picture and turn it into a unique visual element that fits your creative vision.

Filters

A photo's mood or tone can be quickly changed by Canva's built-in filters and design. As an example:
- Use a warm filter to give your photo a cozy, inviting look.
- Apply a black-and-white filter for a classic or dramatic feel.
- Choose high-contrast filters to make colors pop and grab attention.

Manual Adjustments

Canva has tools for making changes by hand for more control. You can change things like:
- **Brightness**: Change how bright or dark the picture looks.
- **Contrast**: Make the difference between light and dark parts bigger to make the picture more interesting.
- **Saturation**: As you change the saturation, you can make colors brighter or less bright.
- **Blur**: To add depth or draw attention to certain parts of an image, add a soft-focus effect.

Transparency

You can make a photo fit in better with your design by changing its transparency. You can use this tool a lot to make backgrounds and overlays.

Photo Effects

People who use Canva Pro can add more complicated effects to their photos, like
- **Background Remover**: With one click, you can get rid of an image's background, leaving only the subject visible for use in different design situations.
- **Duotone**: For a trendy, artistic look, add a two-color overlay.
- **Vignette**: To draw attention to the middle of the picture, add a soft shadow around the sides.

Incorporating Photos into Different Design Types

Because Canva's picture library is so flexible, it can be used for many different design tasks:
1. **Social Media Graphics**: Photos can be the main part of Facebook posts, Instagram posts, or Pinterest pins. Use pictures with a lot of contrast and color to stand out in feeds that are already full.
2. **Marketing Materials**: Pick pictures that help your message stand out for flyers, brochures, and posters. If you pick the right picture, it can help you get your point across and connect with your audience.
3. **Presentations**: Add professional pictures to slides to make presentations that are interesting to look at. Pick pictures that help your points without taking away from the text.
4. **Personal Projects:** For personal projects, you can make invitations, birthday cards, or photo collages with pictures from the library. By adding decorative or themed pictures, you can make the design look better as a whole.

Editing Images: Filters, Cropping, and Adjustments

The picture editing tool in Canva is also very powerful and easy to use. It has a lot more tools than most photo editing apps. I am going to show you how to use Canva's picture maker to make photos that stand out.

How to Crop, Resize, and Flip Image in Canva

First, let's look at how to add your picture to Canva's editor so you can start making changes to it.
Step 1: To begin, open your online browser and go to Canva. From the choice that comes up when you click on the "**Create a design**" button, pick "**Edit photo**."

Step 2: Upload the photo from your PC and click on the Edit photo option.

Step 3: After you upload your picture, a project window will show up. Now you can use Canva's image editor to make changes to it.

Crop Images in Canva

By cutting out parts of the picture that aren't important, cropping lets you focus on the main subject of the picture. Choose the picture in the project window and click on the Crop button at the top to crop it out.

Next, change the frame around the picture to crop it. Last, click "**Done**" to keep the changes.

Besides this, you can also crop images into shapes using the Elements tab.

Resize Images in Canva

You can crop your picture in Canva, but you can also change the size of it to a certain size. Go to the top left and click on the "**Resize**" button. Then, under "**Custom size**," put the width and height you want.

Flip Images in Canva

You can also flip pictures in Canva's image editor to see them from a different angle. To do that, pick the picture in the project window and click the Flip button to make it look horizontal or vertical.

How to Apply Filters in Canva

There are basic editing tools in Canva, but there are also some cool effects you can use on your photos. How to do it.

Step 1: In the photo editor, choose the picture you want to edit and click on the **Edit Image** button.

Step 2: Scroll down to the Filters area in the menu that shows up on the left. Clicking on any of the filters will apply it. You can also change the filter's intensity by double-clicking on it.

Instead, you can use a few adjustment tools to improve the picture by hand. To do that, click the **Edit image** button in the upper left corner and then go to the Adjust section. To make it bigger, click the **"See all"** button next to it.

To make your picture more interesting, you can change things like color, contrast, saturation, clarity, and more by hand here.

How to Remove Background from Image in Canva

No longer do you need a brush and an eraser to get rid of the background in a picture. With just a few clicks, Canva makes it easy to get rid of the background from your picture. Pick out the background you want to get rid of, and then click the Edit image button at the top. Now, from the list, pick the Background Remover option.

That will get rid of the background.

After the removal, you can add elements and writing to your picture to make it more interesting.

How to Add Elements and Text in Canva

Any photo editing app will let you crop and add filters to an image, but Canva stands out because it has a huge library of elements and text styles that you can use to make your photos look more professional.

Add Elements on Image

Step 1: First, go to the left-hand tab that says "**Elements**." This is where you can look through all of Canva's stickers, graphics, photos, charts, and other things.

Step 2: To add the element to your picture, click on it. The above toolbar lets you move, resize, and crop the part after you've added it.

In addition, you can lock the extra element so that you don't move it by mistake. Pick out something you want to lock, and then click on the lock icon in the upper right corner.

The trash icon next to an element lets you get rid of it.

How to Download Edited Photo

You'll need to download your picture after you're done editing it. The steps below will show you how to download it. To download your picture, click the "**Download**" button in the top right corner and choose the format you want from the drop-down menu under "**File type**." Last, get your picture by clicking the **Download** button.

Crop an Image into a Shape on Canva Web

Here's how to use Canva in your web browser to turn a picture into a shape. **Step 1:** First, go to the left and click on the **Elements** tab. Scroll down until you see "**Frames.**" Then, tap "**See All**" and pick the **shape** you like. The frame with the selected shape will be added to the design.

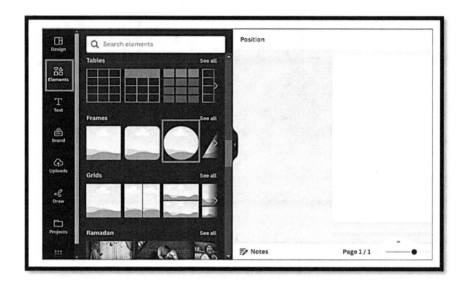

Step 2: Pick out the **frame** and click on the **Uploads tab** on the left. **Upload an image** by dragging and dropping it to the frame. The picture will now take the shape of the frame. To make it bigger, you can **drag the four corners**. To move the picture around in the frame, **double-click** on it and make the picture fit however you want.

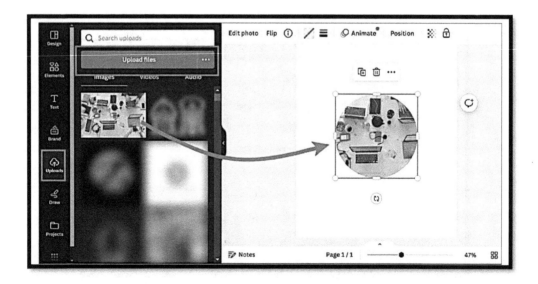

How to Crop an Image into a Shape on Canva Mobile App

In the Canva app for iPhone and Android, you can crop a picture to a shape like this:

Step 1: Open up Canva. In the bottom bar, tap the tab that says "**Elements**." Scroll down until you see "**Frames**." Then, tap "**See All**" and pick any **shape**.

Step 2: The frame will be added to your design. Tap on **Replace** at the bottom and **add the image** you want to crop.

Step 3: The picture will now fit into the frame. To make it bigger, you can **drag the four corners**. If you want to move the picture inside the frame, **double-tap** on it and move it around until it fits.

You can change the cropped picture even more by adding filters, making animations, adding other effects, or changing the transparency.

How to Use Icons in Canva

Step 1 - Create a New Design

Go to Canva and sign in. Then, in the upper right area, click on **Create a Design.** This will bring up a list of templates to use right away. The **Facebook Cover** template is what we'll use. Your work space will be the new window that pops up. You can pick a design that goes with your style here. Either click on a design on the left side panel or type a word into the search bar to do this. I chose to use a **Finance Facebook Cover** template. If you click on "**See all,**" you can see the covers that are offered in each category.

You will see a small crown on some templates if you use the **free version of Canva**. Canva Pro Version is the only way to use these. On the left, click on the template you want to use. This is now going to load on your screen.

Step 2 - Upload your Icons to Canva

Click on the **Uploads** icon on the left side of the screen, then click on the **Upload Media** button. To post more than one icon, hold down **Ctrl and click** on them to select them all. Select the pictures you want, and then click "**Open.**" You can also post SVG files, but I only put up **PNG** files. When you work with SVG files, you can change the colors, but not when you work with PNG files. You can change **Contrast, Brightness**, and a lot more with PNG files, though. In the **Uploads** panel, your icons will now show up on the left.

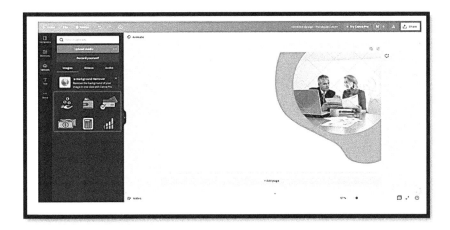

Step 3 - Use Uploaded Icons in Canva

Once the icons are uploaded, all you have to do is click on one to add it to your template. It will be added every time you click on an icon.

Resize, Crop, and Reposition Icon

To change the size, **click and drag** a corner handle to move it in or out. You can also move the icon by **clicking and dragging** it around. **Click and drag** the lines in the middle of the icon's top, bottom, and sides to crop it. The **Crop** option is also in the toolbar at the top of the screen. There will be two boxes around the icon. The one is the original size while the second is the cropping box. **Click + drag** to adjust the crop size then click **Done** at the top.

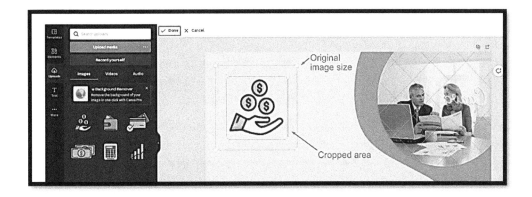

Flip Icon Horizontally or Vertically

Also on the top toolbar is the option to **flip** the image **Horizontally** or **Vertically**.

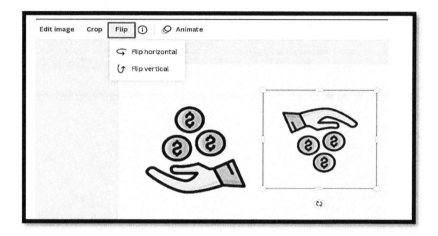

Edit the Icon Image

If you click on **Edit image** at the top, a side panel will open with a range of editing options. You can even add your icon to a mockup like we did in the image below as an example. That's really cool.

To get back to the icons you uploaded, all you have to do is click on **Edit Image** again.

Image Position Options

To align the icons to the page use the **Position** settings found top right.

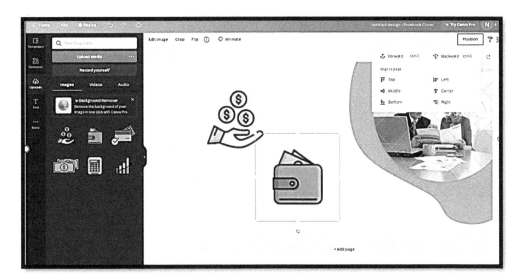

Here you will be able to move a selected icon **forward** (up one layer) or **Backward** (down one layer). This is especially great for placing one icon or image on top of or behind another image.

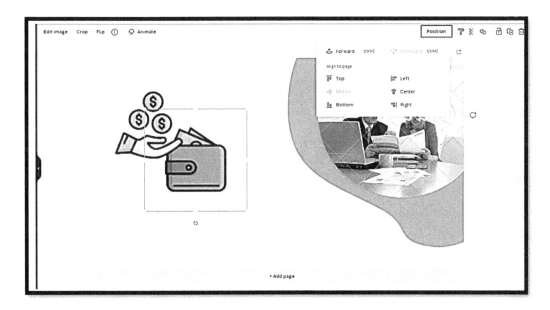

If you click on more than one icon, more options will be added to the **Position** menu. This is where the **Tidy up Feature** lets you make sure the icons are all spaced out properly.

Before you change the size and position of your pictures, you might want to group them together. This choice is also possible when more than one icon is chosen.

Additional Editing Options

The next option is the Copy style. You can copy and paste a format from one text or picture to another with this tool. The first icon in the picture below was changed, and then the **Copy Style** button was clicked. The second icon was then given this style.

The remaining options include:
- **Transparency -** change the transparency of the icon
- **Link -** where you can add a hyperlink
- **Lock -** lock the icon from being edited
- **Duplicate -** duplicate the icon
- **Delete -** delete the icon

Animate the Icons

Did you know that Canva lets you make the icons move? Here is where you can have fun and make material that stands out. Click **Animate** in the menu at the top. On the left side, you'll see the **animate** choices. **Photo Animations** will make the chosen icon move. All of the things on the page will move when you use **Page Animations. Photo Animations** was what I used. Move your cursor over the choices while an icon is selected to see a quick look at them. Click on the image to pick it out and add it. When you click on **Downloads**, this will be saved as an **MP4**. Try out all of the different choices to get the best results with your icons. The animation you picked will show up in the toolbar at the top. Click on **Remove animation** in the bottom left corner of the **animate** panel to get rid of it.

Use the text options in Canva to finish off your template design. Click **Share > Download** to save your project. This is the last step. This choice will change based on the version you're using. Keep in mind that I didn't add the motion, which is why the **File type** says "**PNG**." There is a drop-down button that you can use to change the file type.

If you use the **Free Version**, the file will have a watermark like the one below. The watermark shows up every time a Canva template is used.

The watermark will not be on your design if you use **Canva Pro**. With the Free Version, you can share on social media, but there is a logo on the posts.

CHAPTER 7

DESIGN FEATURES AND TRICKS

Understanding Layer Management

In Canva, you have to arrange things in your design area before you can work with layers. Every part, like text, pictures, shapes, or backgrounds, has its own surface area. These steps will help you work with layers: Layers are stacked on top of each other like paper. What parts appear in front of or behind other parts depends on which layers are in what order. The order of the layers can be changed by moving things forward or backward. To move something up or down in the stack, select it and use the toolbar or right-click menu. This will let you set up the levels. That lets you decide how things look when they meet and interact with each other. You can turn more than one thing into a single unit by grouping its parts. This makes it easier to keep track of designs that are very complicated because you can move or change many parts at once without having to change where each one is put. You can't make mistakes when you lock layers. You can still see locked layers, but you can't pick them or change them until they are unlocked. Making changes to finished parts in this way keeps them safe from being changed without permission. You can remove or show layers to focus on certain parts of your design or to clear your desk for a short time while you work on other parts of it. Layers in templates are already set up in a way that makes it easy to change them. Every part of the design, like the words, pictures, and colors, can be seen and changed so that it fits your style. To make designs that are well-organized and look good with others, you need to learn how to use layers in Canva. Plus, you have full control over where things are put and how they are shown in your compositions.

Finding Layers in Canva

1. The design you want to work on should be open when you click on it in the **Recent Designs** area of Canva Home.

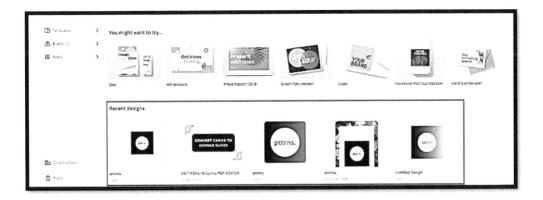

2. If you haven't started already, click the "**Create a design**" button and choose a design to work on first. You can also make your own picture by hitting the "**Custom size**" button.

3. If you already have a plan, skip this step. You should start from scratch if you make a new one, though, and use one of the free templates in the Design panel of the Editor panel to save time.

If you go to the levels panel after the design is done, you can change the levels. You can do this in a number of ways:
By right-clicking on the design:
1. To start, find the picture and click on it.
2. You can see more options when you right-click on it after you've picked it.
3. Now, click on **Layer** and choose **Show Layers** from the menu that comes up.

4. If you did it right, the Layers panel should be on the left.

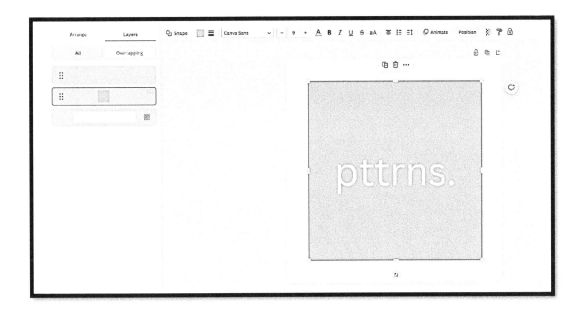

By clicking on Position:
1. Once you've added the design to the board, click on it to pick it.
2. This will show you a list of options at the top.
3. Now, click on **Position** from the list of options. The Arrange board will show up on the left.

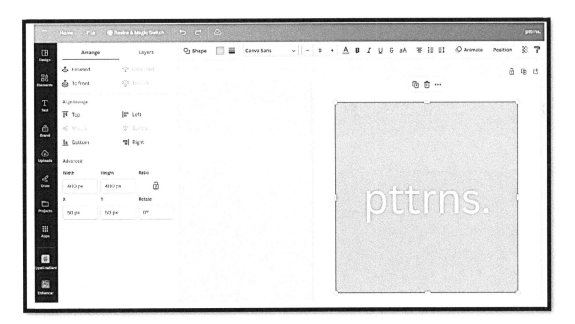

4. To see the Layers panel, click on **Layers** to the right of **Arrange**.

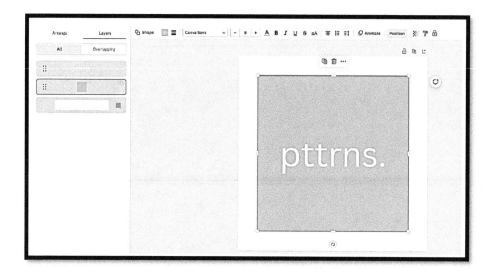

Tip: The above ways can take a long time if you're working on a big plan. They fixed this by adding a keyboard shortcut: **Alt + 1.** The Layers panel shows up right away on the left when you press this.

Arranging Layers in Canva

Setting up levels is probably the easiest thing to do, thanks to the levels panel. This is how you put layers in order:

1. Click on the layer you want to rearrange in the Layers panel.
2. Click and hold on a layer, then move it up or down the panel as needed.

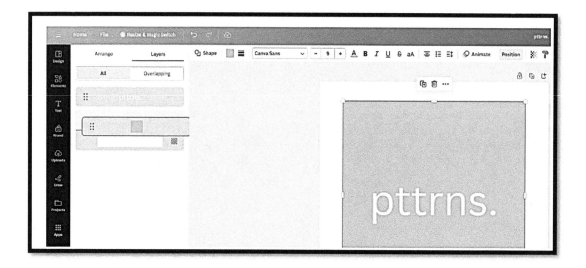

Tip: It can take a while to change each layer one at a time. If you hold down the **Shift** key and click on several areas at once, it will be easier to do. The layers will be picked out and can be changed at the same time if you do it right.

Overlay Images

1. To start, go to Canva and sign in with your passwords. Go to Canva Home, then go to **Recent Designs**. Click on the project you want to work on now.
2. If you haven't already, go to the home screen, click on "**Create a design**," and then choose a design to start.
3. Once the new or old design is loaded, go to the left-hand **Editor panel** and click on **Uploads**. Click the **Upload Files** button if you haven't already, and make sure the file doesn't have a background while you do so.

4. First, click on the picture to get rid of the background. Then use the options above to "**Edit the image.**" The **Effects panel** will then appear on the left, where you can click on the **BG removal tool.**

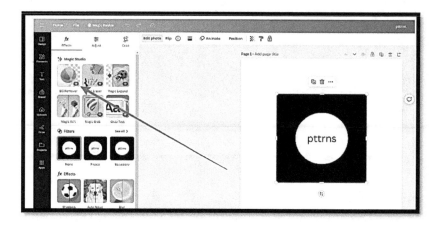

5. You can get rid of the background for free with online tools like remove.bg if you can't get Canva Pro.

Overlay Images in Canva: Demonstration

You can start putting the picture on top now that everything is ready. We made a simple example with steps that can be used as a starting point for all of them because the effects are different and can be used to make an infinite number of designs.

1. Start by adding a background to the blank canvas. It could be a design, text, picture, or frame.
2. Now go to the **Editor panel** and click on **Uploads**. When the **Uploads box** shows up, click on the picture whose background you want to add to the painting.
3. Once the picture is added, right-click on the element at the top to see more options for where it should go. Now, click on Layer and then on **Send to forward or backward**, depending on what you need to do.

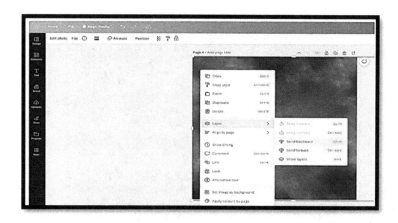

4. Next, change the levels of transparency for the elements by using the **Transparency tool** located above the editor. Then, change the amount of transparency for each picture with the scale.

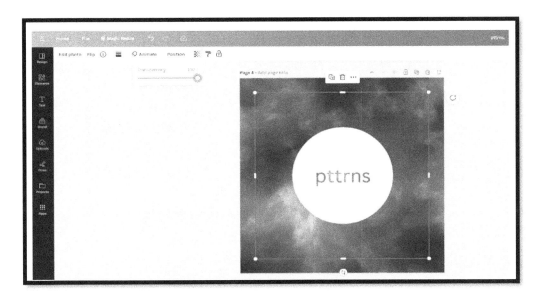

5. To make your design even better, add picture effects and cool styles. If you want to take your art idea further, you can choose parts from a huge library of icons, vectors, and drawings.

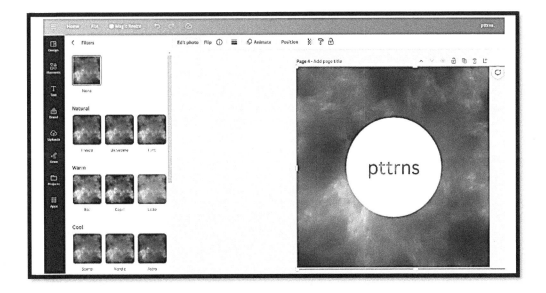

6. Click on **Share** in the top right corner when you're done making changes. Now, click on **Download** from the list that showed up. After that, pick the type of file you want to download and press the **Download** button.

Applying and Customizing Filters

Computer

1. Click the photo or video you want to edit.
2. On the editor's menu, click on either **Edit Photo or Edit Video**. On the side panel, you'll see the picture editing options that are offered.
3. Under **Filters**, click **See All**.
4. Pick out a filter to use it.
5. Drag the **Intensity** scale below the filter you've chosen to change how strong the filter is. You can move the scale to the right to make it stronger or to the left to weaker.
6. Click on a different filter to switch between them.
7. Choose "**None**" to get rid of the filter that was applied.
8. Click anywhere to save the changes and close the filter row.

Mobile

1. Click on the picture or video you want to edit.
2. From the editor toolbar below, tap **Filter**. You may have to swipe through the options below to see it.
3. Pick the option you want to use. To see all the settings, swipe through the options.
4. Pick out a filter to use it.
5. Drag the Intensity scale below the filter you've chosen to change how strong the filter is. You can move the scale to the right to make it stronger or to the left to weaker.
6. Tap on a different filter to switch between them.
7. Choose "**None**" to get rid of the filter that was applied.
8. Press on any spot to save and close the filter table.

Advanced Canva Filter Techniques

Using Multiple Filters

One great thing about Canva effects is that you can use more than one tint on the same picture. These tools let you add effects to your photos that are both unique and beautiful. This can help your photos stand out. One filter at a time can be used in Canva. To add another, just click "**Add Filter**" after adding the first filter. You can do this another time or times until you get the result you want. Remember that adding too many effects to a picture can make it look fake and unattractive. Be careful not to use too many filters, and try out different mixes until you find the right one.

Creating Custom Filters

Canva also lets you make frames, which is another cool way to make your photos look different. First, give your picture the effects you want to use. This is what you need to make your filter. Choose everything you want, and then click "Adjust" to go to the advanced scale. To get the look you want, you can change how each filter is set up here. Once you're done making your filter, click the "Save Filter" button to save it. You can use the same tint on other pictures from now on, which will save you time and work.

Working with Gradients and Transparency

Creating Gradient

Find the "**Elements**" option above the "**Uploads**" feature and click it after you've posted the picture you want to. In the search bar that appears, type "**gradient**" and press the **Enter** key on your keyboard to begin the search.

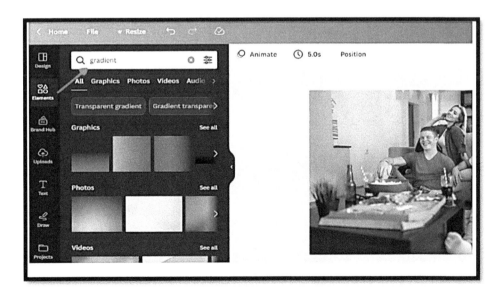

You can pick from a few different color options that Canva gives you. It's easy to add a color; just look through the choices and click on the one you want. You can click and hold on the gradient's corners with your mouse or keyboard when you're done with it. You can fill in the blanks by dragging the corners in the way you want. You can change the picture in the box in the top right corner of the screen. To get to the screen if you can't find it, click the "**More**" button.

Lower the Transparency

To make a gradient solid color less see-through, you can change how powerful it is. It will become less clear, which will make the color look denser and firmer.

This answer to "**transparent gradient canva**" is the right one. Now you can choose a color. Click on "**Position**" in the menu at the top right of the program's screen once you've made your choice.

The "**backward**" button lets you move the gradient back one layer at a time until it's where you want it to be. To get the layers in the right order, you may need to click "backward" more than once. When you click on the gradient colors in the top left corner of your Canva window, they will show up. Then you can pick the color design you like best.

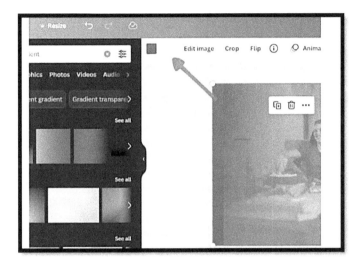

You need to download your picture when you're done making it. To do so, you must find the "**Share**" button, which is typically in the top-right section of the screen.

When you click on it, you'll be asked to pick a file to download. After that, the picture will be sent to your device.

How to Make a Gradient Text in Canva

1. **Click on Create a Design**
- First, you have to make a custom gradient in Canva. Then you can add a free gradient to text. If you want to use the tools that come with Canvas, you have to pick the gradient colors and levels of strength by hand.

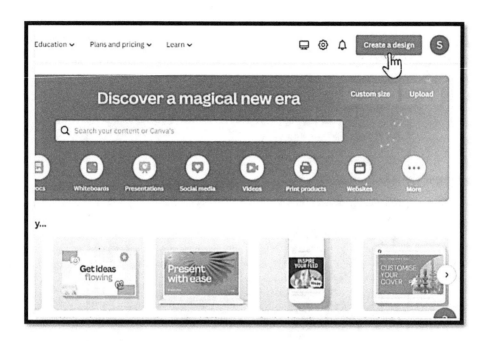

- After you log in, look for the "**Create a design**" button and tap it.

2. **Head to Element Option**

- After that, on the left, you'll see a menu bar or sidebar.

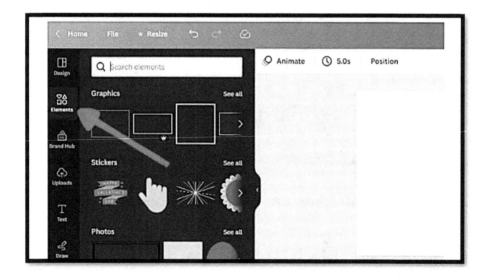

- In this case, find the "**Elements**" option in the tab and click on it. This will bring up a list of all the different parts that make up the page.

3. **Type "Gradient" and Choose Color**

- Type "**gradient**" into the search bar next. Next, pick a free design.

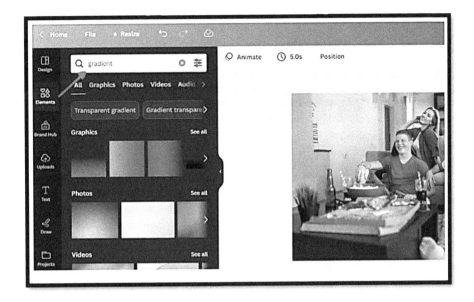

- Find the two-color options and make your choice from there.
4. **Download in PNG Format**
- To save your new file, click "**Save**" and pick **PNG** as the file type.
- Now that you have a gradient, you can make a text effect.
5. **Launch a New Page**
- To get to a new page, click on the "**Create new design**" icon.
- There is now a blank space for you to work on.
6. **In Elements, Search "Letter a frame"**
- Pick out the elements you want to work on. If you type and then click on "**Letter a frame**," you can move on.
- To pick out a letter, just click on it and hold down the mouse button. After that, move the letter where you want it and let go of the mouse button.
- You would have to do the same things for each letter that you need.
7. **Add Your Gradient File**
- Put in the PNG file that has your color in it. This file can then be dragged into each letter to add the gradient effect.

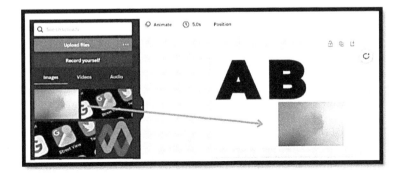

- To make the gradient image size go all the way to the edges of the page, double-click on each letter and change its size.
8. **Change the Position**
- Next is to change the position.

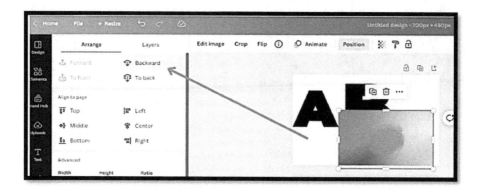

Choose the gradient, then press the Position button in the upper right corner and pick "**Backward**."

Make a Gradient in Canva on Text with a Mobile

You can now find out how to add a color to text on your phone using Canva.
1. **Access the Canva Dashboard**

First, please go to the Canva home page and look for the icon that looks like a plus sign in the bottom right corner of your screen. If you click on this button, you'll be taken to different areas of Canva where you can make new designs or projects.

2. **Click the Facebook Post Option**

Please pick or click on the "**Facebook Post**" template you see.

3. **Go to the Photos Option and Type Gradient**

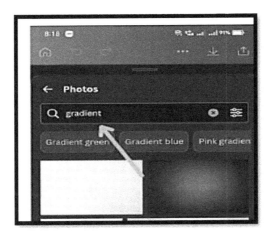

Click on the "**+**" sign one more time to keep working on the job. This should show you a list of choices. To find the right pictures, go to "**Photos**" and then "**Gradient**." On Canva, find the color picture you want. When you find it, click on it to pick it. Then, use your mouse or keyboard to drag your gradient picture to the whole template you're working with.

4. **Click the "Text" option to Add the Text**

The next thing you need to do is type in the words you want the gradient to appear on. To do this, put the words where you want the gradient effect to show up.

Pick up the "+" sign when you see it. Now, look for the "**Text**" button. This will show a text editor window with some fonts and text styles. Choose the type of text you want to use, like a paragraph or a heading. Pick a font from the ones that are available now. Canva has a lot of fonts to choose from, so take your time and find the right one for your project. Choose a font and then add the words to the picture. Then, click and drag the sides of the text box to make it the right size. Type the words you want to use into the text box. You can also change the structure in any other way you see fit. You now have a font and a color. After that, the words need to be given color.

5. **Change Text Color to Set Transparency**

Make the words white. To change how see-through the text is, select the text box and set the transparency level to 40%.

6. **Download in PNG Format**

Save the picture as a PNG file.

7. **Create a New Canva Template**

Now make a new template that is blank.

8. Upload Your New PNG File

Find the PNG file you just made in the "**Uploads**" section after hitting the "**+**" button and select it. Use the "**resize**" option to make the PNG file the right size after you're done uploading it.

9. **Remove Background**

Select "**Effects**" and then click "**Background Remover**." Give it some time to finish. You now know how to use Canva to change the color of text on a white background. You need to change the text in the last few steps to make the pattern better.

10. **Crop Your Text and Use Adjust Feature**

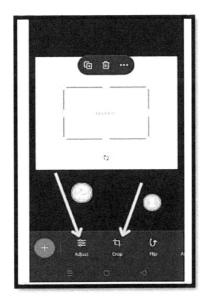

You have to crop the text, click the "**Adjust**" button in the menu, and use the scales to change the colors.

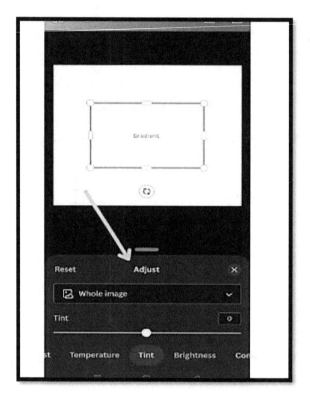

Create a Gradient Background in Canva

1. Pick out the style you want to use after clicking "**Create Design**." Pick out a YouTube clip template as an example.
2. To find gradient graphics, click on "**elements**" and type "**gradient**."
3. To view more options and pick a gradient you like, click "**see all**."
4. Change the colors and the size of the transition to fit the whole picture. The pattern is easy to flip if you need to.

Make Gradient Background on the Mobile

1. **Click the "+" button**
- For a gradient background, find the plus sign (**+**) in the bottom left corner of the designer.
- To add a gallery, text, or other things to your project, just taps this button. What you see are the choices.
2. **Look for the Background Option**
- First, swipe left and right until you see Background. After that, tap it to change the background. If you can't find it, swipe to get to the "**More**" button. It ought to have the "**Background**" option inside it.

The color tile is below the search bar. To change the color of a part, you need to find it. Once you find the color tile, all you have to do to use it is tap on it. To get back to your design, swipe down on the part of the screen. This will take you back to the main view, where you can get back to work on your project. These steps will help you change the color of the gradient background.

3. Locate the Palette Icon

To get to the color tools in Canva, press the Palette button.

- When you click this, a screen will show up where you can choose a color or make your own.
4. **Tap the "+" Icon**
- Click on the plus sign (+) to open it.
- This should give you a list of the colors that are available right now.
5. **Select Your New Color**
- As soon as you pick a new color, click "**Save**" to save it on your device. You can also click "**Download**" and choose the kind of file you want to get.

Make a Gradient Shape in Canva

1. Pick the template when you click "**Create a design**."
2. Go to the Elements section and look for "**Gradient**."
3. Look at the graphs and click "**See All**."
4. You can choose from different shapes when you click on "**Gradient Shape**."
5. Last, make the gradient shapes bigger or smaller so they fit the whole picture, and use magic as you like. The pattern is easy to flip if you need to.

Understanding Color Theory

Have you ever thought about how designers and artists pick the colors that go best with each other? They know what color something is. Science and art can be useful together in color theory, which helps people pick colors that go well together. A circle with the color spectrum on it was made by Isaac Newton in 1666. This is how the color wheel was made. A color wheel is used to explain color theory. It shows how colors are related to each other. Color balance means that two colors look good together. Artists and designers use these to alter how things appear or feel. You can use a color wheel to find color balance by following the rules for how to pair colors. With color combinations, you can figure out where to put each color to get results that look good. Color wheels come in two types. Artists use the RYB (red, yellow, blue) color wheel all the time to help them mix paint colors. The RGB color wheel mixes light like on a computer or TV screen. It's made to be used online. RGB stands for "red, green, and blue." Because Canva is an online tool, its color wheel is an RGB wheel.

Color Combinations

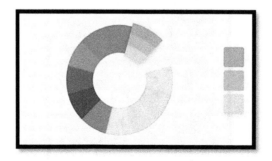

Monochromatic

There are three different shades, tones, and tints of the same base color. Comes in a soft and classic color mix. This group of colors goes well together and can be used in lots of different ways. It's also simple to use in design projects.

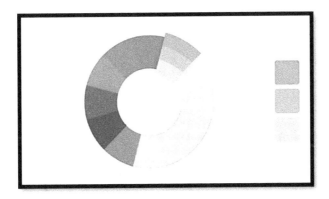

Analogous

There are three colors next to each other on the color wheel. There are times when this color scheme is great, and times when it's too much. To make a color scheme look better, use the other colors to draw attention to the main color.

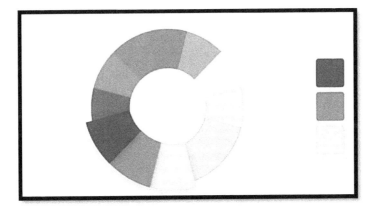

Triadic

There are equal amounts of three colors on the color wheel. There is a lot of difference between these colors, but not as much as between the complementary colors. It can be used in more scenarios now because of this. This mix makes bright and bold color schemes.

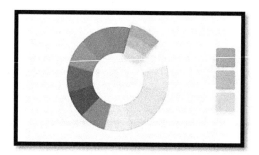

Complementary

Two colors on the color wheel that are not next to each other. The contrast and effect of these colors are strong. When put together, they will look softer and stand out more.

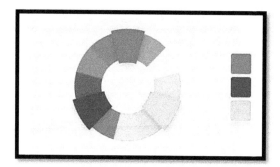

Triadic

There are equal amounts of three colors on the color wheel. There is a lot of difference between these colors, but not as much as between the complementary colors. It can be used in more scenarios now because of this. This mix makes bright and bold color schemes.

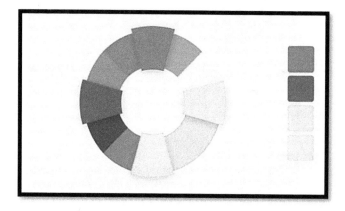

Tetradic

There is an even space between the four colors on the color wheel. To make a tetradic color scheme look good, make one color pop out and use the others to bring it out. Having too many colors makes it harder to keep the order.

Primary, Secondary, And Tertiary Colors

There are 12 main colors on the wheel. Red, orange, yellow, green, spring green, cyan, azure, blue, violet, magenta, and rose make up the RGB color wheel. The color wheel can be broken up into three groups: primary, secondary, and tertiary.

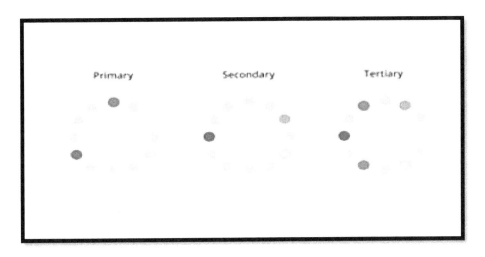

Primary colors: On the RGB color wheel, the primary colors are the ones that, when added together, make white light. There are blue, green, and red shades.
- Colors that are primary on the RYB color wheel are those that can't be mixed with any other color. Blue, yellow, and red are the primary colors.

Secondary colors: These are the colors you get when you mix two primary colors. There are three other colors. These are the colors cyan, magenta, and yellow on the RGB wheel. When you mix red and green, you get a yellow light. When you mix green and blue, you get cyan light. And when you mix blue and red, you get magenta light.
- Red mixed with blue makes purple. Orange is made of red and yellow. And green is made of yellow and blue.

Tertiary colors: When you mix a primary color with a secondary color, you get a tertiary color. There are six tertiary colors. These are the colors on the RGB wheel: blue, rose, chartreuse green, spring green, and chartreuse green.
- Red-orange, yellow-orange, yellow-green, blue-green, blue-violet, and red-violet make up the tertiary colors of the RYB color wheel.

Warm and Cool Colors

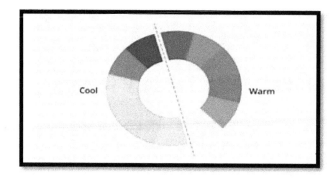

The color wheel can also be split into cool and warm groups. What other word do you use for color temperature? It means how warm or cool a color is. A color wheel usually has a good mix of cool and warm colors. Color psychology says that different color temperatures make us feel various emotions. People say that warm colors make them feel good and give them energy, while cool colors make them feel calm and alone. Tones that are warm range from red to yellow. People say that these colors make them feel warm, like the sun. Cool colors range from blue to green to purple. People say that these colors make them think of cool things, like water.

Shades, tints, and tones

By adding black, gray, and white to a base hue, you can make shades, colors, and tones.
- **Shade:** To make a shade, you mix a base hue with black to make it darker. It gets darker and fuller this way. Some of the shades are too strong and bright.
- **Tint:** To make a tint, you mix a base color with white. This makes the color softer. This can make a color less bright or help make color combinations that are too bright look better.
- **Tones:** To make a tone, mix a base color with black and white (or gray). Like shades, tones are lighter versions of the main color. Tone colors are less likely to look light, and they can show depths that aren't obvious from the base color.

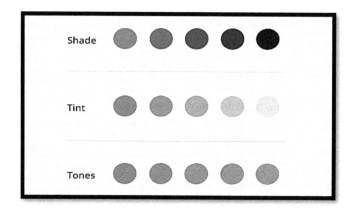

Hue, Saturation, and Luminance

- A **hue** is any color on the color wheel. When you use a color wheel or a color picker, you can change how bright and saturated a color is.
- **Saturation** is a measure of how pure or intense a color is.
- The amount of light or shine in a color is called its **luminance.**

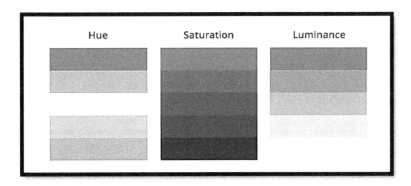

Overview of Color Picker Tool

There is a helpful tool in Canva called the "color picker" that lets you change the colors of design parts and how they look. Here's a rundown of what it can do and how it works:

Accessing the Color Picker Tool

You can use the color picker tool to change any text, shapes, backgrounds, or images that are based on color. When you want to change a color, all you have to do is click on the color tile in the menu next to it.

What the Color Picker Tool Can Do

1. **Color Palette**: The color picker shows a list of base colors and the most recent colors you've used in your work. It's easy to stay on track while you do your job this way.
2. **Custom Colors**: Click on the rainbow-shaped "+" button to make your own colors. This opens a full-color picker where you can change the hue, saturation, and brightness (HSB) or type in exact hex codes to find the right color.
3. **Hex Codes and RGB Values**: It's possible to type the hex code of the color you want into the color picker if you know exactly what color you want. You can change the RGB choices instead to make your color.
4. **Eyedropper Tool**: This tool lets you choose a color from anywhere in your design or load images right away. This helps you accurately match colors to other parts of a design or pictures.

5. **Brand Kit Integration**: If you have Canva Pro, the color choice works with the Brand Kit tool. This makes it simple to find and use your brand colors. This makes sure that everything with your name on it looks the same.

6. **Transparency**: There is also a number for transparency in the color setting. With this, you can change how opaque the color you've chosen is. This can help you make effects with many layers, patterns, or soft backgrounds.

Using the Color Picker Tool

Step 1: First, click on the thing you want to make stand out by changing its color. A box will be put around it.

Step 2: Click on the square of color in the upper left corner. It will show you what color the thing you picked is at the moment.

Step 3: On the left, click on the box with the plus sign in the middle. Pick a new color now.

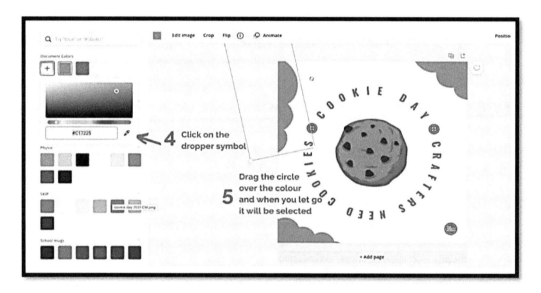

Step 4: Click and hold on the drip sign when it shows up. You can move around this circle that forms.

Step 5: To pick the color, move the circle over the design or the whole screen. You can see the new color in the list of document colors on the left when you let go. The thing you first chose will also be colored in the new color.

Applying and Modifying Colors in Designs

Changing Colors of Design Elements

1. You would like to change one thing. One or more color tiles will show up on the menu above the editor, depending on how many colors the part you chose has.

2. Click on a color's tile to change it. It will show you the colors of your paper and other things. The color themes you've already made will also be shown.

3. If you click on a color in the color panel, that color will be applied to the element you picked.
4. To change the color, click the "**Add a new color**" tile in the color box. Drag the circle to pick a new color. You can put the hex color code here. You may also use slopes.
5. Once you've clicked on the rainbow tile, move your mouse over the part of your design that you want to change color and click the eyedropper icon. Click on the part to add color.

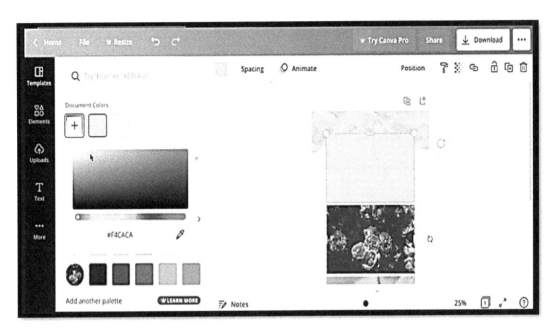

Note: The eyedropper color option is only available in the Canva app for computers and in Google Chrome and Edge.

Change the Color Scheme of Your Canva Design in One Click

Step 1: Select a Template
You can see Canva's library on the home page and choose a useful template from there if you don't already have a project going. Are you more specific about what you want to find? The search bar can help. Click on the template you want and then click on hit **customize this template**.

Step 2: Insert Your Image of Choice
You can change a template in any way you want once you've chosen it, even if it comes with a color scheme. You might want to use layers in Canva if you are working on a very involved project. You don't need to worry about changing the colors of any small parts right now; you can do that later.

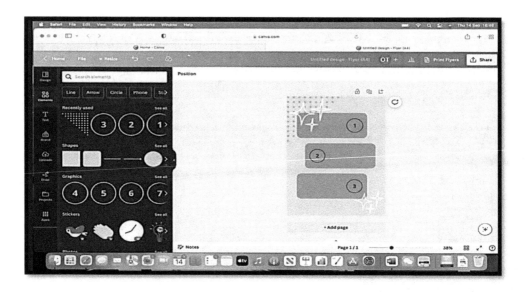

As soon as the whole project is ready, add a picture of the colors you want to use to the design you already have. Adding a picture from your files is easy—just drag and drop it on the project page. You can also pick an old file from the Uploads tab on the left.

Step 3: Apply Your New Colors

Select the picture you want to use as a color scheme guide and right-click on it. Then, select "**Apply colors to page**." The new color scheme from the picture should show up right away in your design.

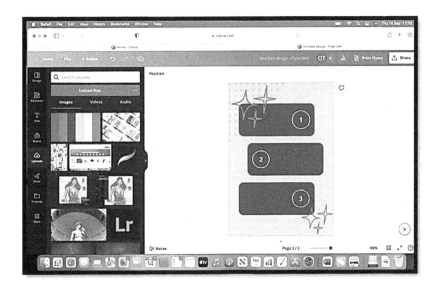

You can use this tool to change anything in Canva that can be changed. There are a lot of elements built into Canva that you can choose from. You can also use outside programs like Adobe Illustrator to make elements that can be changed in color.

Ways You Can Avoid Blurry Canva Designs

1. **Use the Right Canvas Size**

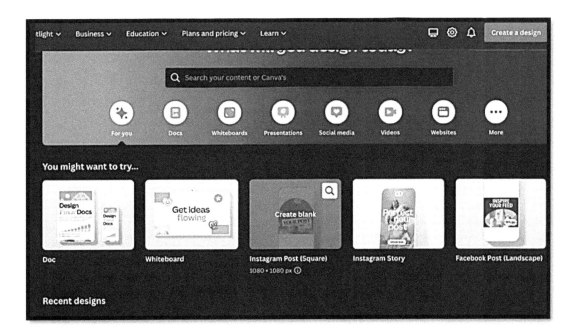

You quickly learn about the different types of canvas, each of which is a different size, once you start using Canva. You'll need to set the canvas's width and height before you can use it. But you can't just pick any board. Whether you use a board that's already out there or make your own, it has to be the right size. Your design will be fuzzy if it isn't. Specifically, don't use numbers that are less than what is suggested. One example is an Instagram post, which is 1080 x 1080 pixels. It will be less clear when you download and share a 400 x 400 px Instagram post. Not sure what size paper to use? You can always look it up, so make sure you know it before you do something. You also shouldn't change the design's size, because that can make it look fuzzy. Remember that this only works for Canva Pro users, since you can't change the size of a picture in the free version. You can make a design bigger with Canva Pro if you finish it and then decide it's too small. This is one reason why you should become a Canva Pro user.

2. Download Your Designs as PNGs

Facebook and Instagram both make pictures smaller, which can make them look hazy. If your drawings are saved as PNG files, even if they have words on them, this won't happen.

How to do it:
- Press the **Share** button.
- Click on **Download**.
- Choose **PNG** from the list of file types.
- Click **Download** after picking out the pages you want to save.

Following this, your picture should be saved to your phone as a PNG file.

3. Download Your Designs as PDFs, Then Convert Them

You can save your drawings as PDFs first and then change them if getting them as PNGs doesn't work. This is very helpful because it keeps the pictures clear when you use a lot of them in your design. When you save your work as a PDF, choose **PDF Print** instead of **PDF Standard**. Make sure your pictures are good enough to print if you want to.

To save your work, go to Share > Download and choose PDF Print as the file type. You can go online and change it to a PNG or JPG file after you've saved it.

4. Avoid Over-Enlarging Elements in Your Design

When you use Canva, you can change the size of your design parts if you need to. When you enlarge things like pictures and graphics too much, they can start to look fuzzy.

5. **Stick to High-Quality Images**

Check that the pictures you use in Canva designs are good (at least 300 PPI). Things will get fuzzy if you do anything else. You don't have to pay a professional shooter to get good pictures. Instead, you can find photography websites where you can get pictures without having to pay for the rights to use them.

6. Review Your Designs Before Downloading Them

Make sure your pictures are ready to use one last time before you save them. Is your subject too little or too much? Are the pictures you've taken very clear? Do some of your parts look a little wonky? Think about these things. esides going over your plan, make sure you pick the right file type. If everything looks good, you can now download what you made.

Key Takeaways

- Use the right area size in Canva to keep your pictures from being fuzzy. Don't choose smaller sizes, and always check the sizes twice to make sure they fit.
- Keep your pictures sharp by saving them as PNG files. This is especially important if they have text in them.
- Save your drawings as PDFs first and then change them if they don't work as PNGs. Pick PDF Print if you want good prints.

Sometimes, after putting a lot of work into a Canva project, it comes out blurry. Don't worry—if you use the right paper size, save your drawings as PNGs or PDFs, and pick good pictures, this won't happen. Follow these tips to improve your Canva project and fix any fuzzy designs you may have made.

CHAPTER 8

ADVANCED CANVA TECHNIQUES

Animation and Video Features

If you use film and music in your marketing materials and on social media, more people will notice you and follow you. Lots of people like videos and posts that move around on social media sites like Facebook. This is because people can understand movement better than still pictures. If you can make images that move, it will help your business.

Creating presentations

It keeps getting better at making presentations as Canva adds more tools. You can now play games and make presentations that look great for work or fun. These are great for lessons, training, Zoom calls, or just showing something in a fun way. There are different layouts you can use in Canva, but we'll stick with the first one, **Presentations (16:9).** If you click on this option, a new show template will appear:

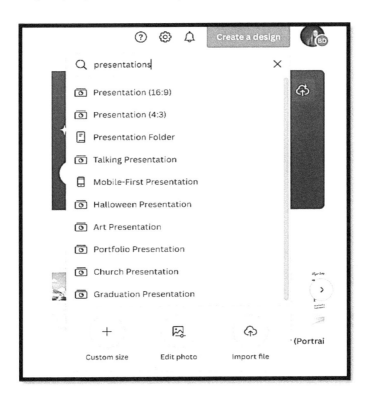

You may have seen that the pages of videos run along the bottom of the screen instead of under each other. This is how you can see how the pages will fit together:

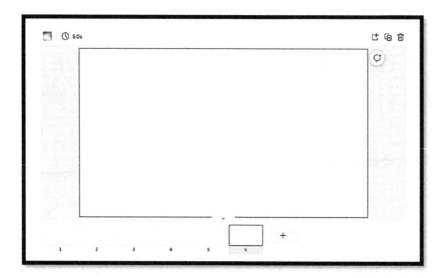

You can make your own show with elements, images, and shapes, or you can pick one of the many templates on the left and change it to fit your needs. You can use the search bar at the top to find one that fits your niche. When you click on many of the templates, you'll see that they have more than one page. You can either click "**Apply all x pages**" or pick and choose which ones to add. After the fact, if you change your mind, you can delete them one by one:

I've put all of the pages on the screen to show this. You can now see them lined up at the bottom. Like any other Canva template, I can change the text, pictures, and colors on each page to make it fit my brand. Click styles on the left to choose the colors you want for your brand if you have the PRO version. After that, click the button that says "Apply to all pages" to finish. During the whole talk, your brand will be shown:

Now things are starting to look very different. You can choose how to show your work after you've changed the pictures, added the information you need, and taken out any pages you don't need.

You can pick one of four things on the Present tab:

- **Standard**: This mode lets you watch the show whenever you want and move on to the next page when you're ready. The screen is also full of it.
- **Autoplay**: You decide how long each page plays for. It will then go through your show by itself. It is also set to PC mode.
- **Presenter view**: The presenter view has two doors that can be opened. You can move the first window to where you want it on the screen you will be looking at.

With the second one, you can give your viewers information. **You can see your show's pages and notes that will help you:**

- **Present and record**: This is my favorite because it lets you give your talk and record it at the same time. It works great for lessons that have already been recorded because it has a small recording of you in the corner. Once you pick it up, it will take you to the recording room.

Here is where you can make sure the camera and mic are set up right before you record. With this option, the notes will be on the right and the pages will run along the bottom, but your short movie will only be shown in the corner of the full-screen view. After you are done recording, you can share a link to the show or save it to your computer to watch later. Another thing I love about presentations is the computer shortcuts. Canva now has typing tools that add little pictures all over the page. **Check this out: While you talk, hold down one of these keys:**

- *C*: Confetti
- *D*: Drum roll
- *Q*: Quiet emoji
- *U*: Curtains fall
- *O*: Bubbles
- *B*: Blur

- *M*: Mic drop

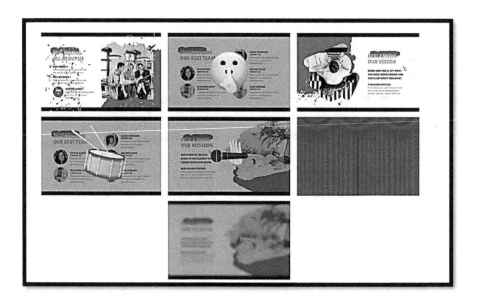

Adding graphics to presentations makes them even more fun. Now, let's look at how to change your social graphics and add music and video, which should help you get more attention.

How to Add and Edit Audio

There are a lot of people who add music to their designs for video sites like Instagram, TikTok, YouTube, and more. But sometimes you might not want to hear the sounds that came with the movie. You might have also made a movie without any sound. In the end, you can add music to make it more interesting for people to watch. Once your image is open in Canva, you can find the **Audio** and **Video** options on the left side of the screen. Scroll down to the bottom; in the very far left corner is the **Apps** tab:

I will talk about how sound works, where to find different sound files, and how to add them to your Canva design.

1. Videos and sounds will be at the top of the list when you click on Apps. They will show up in your menu if you click on each one individually.
2. In this part, we'll talk about how to add sound to your design, so click on Audio to see the search results.

There are buttons below the search bar that can help you find different types of songs. That being said, you can scroll down to see recently used or other well-known audio files.

3. Next, move your mouse over the picture icon to see a play button appear. This will play the sound file. Click this to hear the sound before you add it to your work.
4. Once you find a sound you like, you can add it to the design. It will show up at the top when a part of the sound is played. To change this, drag the blue bar along the sound.

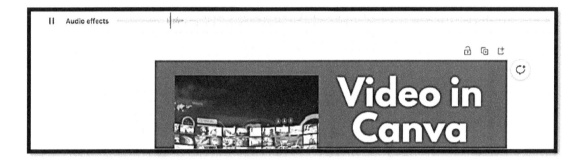

5. In this case, the recording part that will play is only five seconds long. To change the size, you need to change the time frame of the design, not the music file. The sound will play for a certain amount of time every time. Click the trash can icon in the top right corner to get rid of the sound and make the design longer:

6. It'll be the same bar at the top again. You can change the time in this box and press **Enter** to change how long the picture is. It's always 5 seconds long.

7. You can now add your sound again, and it will sound great:

You can only add one sound file at a time. If you want to add another one, just drop it in. It will replace the old one. Also, click on the speaker button in the top right corner to change how loud the sound is. We'll look at how to add and change a movie next.

How to Add and Edit Video

Canva has a lot of great lessons. There is a good chance that you will find what you need. You can also add movies, change them, and get rid of the backgrounds. But I do want to make it clear that this is a **PRO** tool. If you want to add a movie to a Canva template, go to a new or used template and click on the Upload tab on the left. You can now send pictures and movies from your computer. Once you've added a movie, click on it in the upload area, and it will be added to your template. The choices in the top bar let you change it from here: This app will show up on the left side of the screen when you click on the Edit video tab. You can change your video's shade, color, brightness, and contrast on the right.

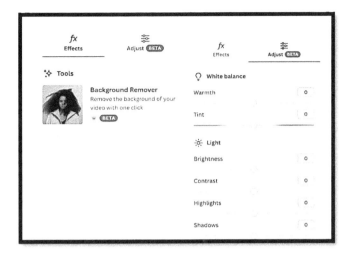

Watch this movie both before and after you use the Background Remover app. This is the old movie with all the background:

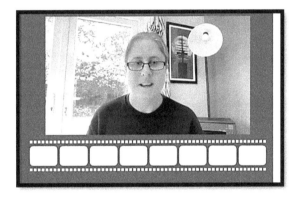

This is what it looks like after the background is gone:

Now I can add this to any design, no matter what color the background, grid, or frame is. This will make my movie and design look better. I can also add a picture to frames and squares while getting rid of other things. I can now trim or cut movies. Most of the time, I want to get rid of that part at the end that makes it look unfinished, like when I reach over to click "**End**" after recording. To do this, I can pull the purple lines at the beginning and end of the video in the top bar and then click "**Done.**" This will shorten your movie, and the box on the left will show you the difference. It says 9.1 seconds right now:

You can also pick between two Playback. One lets you loop the movie forever, which means it will keep playing until you stop it. Setting the movie to play itself means you don't have to press play every time you want to watch it:

You can also change the video's size by bringing these white areas closer together on top of the screen. You can get rid of things or people in the background this way. Turn or flip the video one last time, and then animate it like you would any other template or element.

How to Add Animation

You could use animation instead of film. If you don't want to record a video or can't find one that works for you on Canva, you can add motion to your design to turn it into an MP4 file. It will still have movement and video for social media. There are several ways to add animation and move different parts of your design up and down.

The following can be animated:
- The entire design is one
- Individual text boxes
- Individual elements
- Individual images and videos

If you choose a different part of your picture, different choices will show up on the left. Click "**Animate**" each time you choose a picture, text box, or feature. A new graphics box with two columns will show up on the left. One will have the thing you chose, and the other will have the whole page. You can pick from:

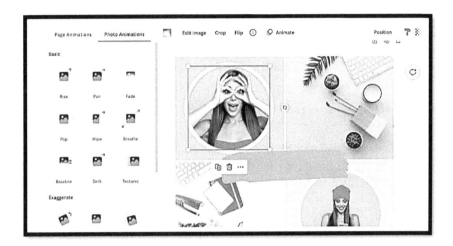

You can see how a motion will look in your design by moving your mouse over one of the boxes. The same thing will happen if you click on **Page Animations** and move your mouse over them. The motion will now be used on the whole design, though. The animations for elements, pictures, and videos are very much the same, but pictures and videos have three more choices. You'll also see these at the bottom, which are only for pictures and videos:

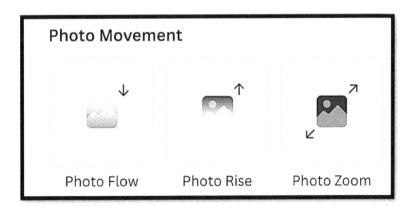

A few changes have been made to the text boxes. You now have more choices, such as the Typewriter look. These are unique to the writing and can make your work stand out:

You can add moving parts to your design by using dynamic features and stickers. This whole list can be found in the part about elements. This can also be used to find music and film.

Recording Directly into Canva

This is a great tool that can save you a lot of time when you want to record something and add it to a Canva template. Other times, you'd need to go to a different site or take a picture and upload it to your computer before you could add it. The record straight tool gets rid of all of this and is also very simple to use. **To find the function, you have to be on the design where you want to add the recording. I made the following mock-up:**

I want to add a small movie to Canva below the text movie. Find the menu on the left side of the screen and select "**Uploads**." This is where you'll find the buttons to Upload Files and Record yourself. Choose:

It will bring up a new window with your template in the background and a small picture of you in the bottom left corner:

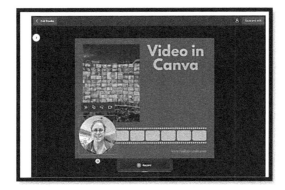

There are four choices above this box. They are:
- **Filters & effects**

Here you can change how your movie looks. For now, there is only one benefit, and that is making the skin smooth:

- **Change shape**

This way, you can pick a movie that is either round or square.

- **Mirror Camera**

With this function, the camera is turned around so that any writing or text can be seen correctly.

- **Turn camera off**

With this option, you can only record sound and not the camera. Take a look at this guide and leave everything as it is. Just click the record button at the bottom. After three, two, and one counts, it will start recording on its own. After that, a red circle with the word "**RECORDING**" in it will appear to let you know you are live. And then press "Done." The movie will be processed for you. After that, click the "**Save and exit**" tab in the top right corner. The video will be added to your plan. Just drag and drop it where you want it to be. After you save and download your design, you can use it right away. Being able to record right into Canva is a useful tool that saves a lot of time. It also has a library of movies that you can use or add your own.

Creating Infographics

Infographics are pictures that show data in a way that is appealing and simple to understand. With an easy-to-use design tool like Canva, you can turn complicated numbers or text into pictures that are simple to understand. Yes, you can use Canva to make professional-looking charts even if you don't know much about design. With Canva's drag-and-drop tools, you can easily edit an already-made infographic or design one from scratch. **Here are the steps you need to follow to make a chart on Canva.**

1. **Sign Up or Log In to Canva**

You'll need to sign up for or log in to Canva before you can make a chart. You can use your email, Facebook, or Google account to sign up.

2. **Create Your Canvas**

Click **Create a Design** in the upper right area of the home page after logging in. On the next screen, look for "infographic" in the search bar that shows up.

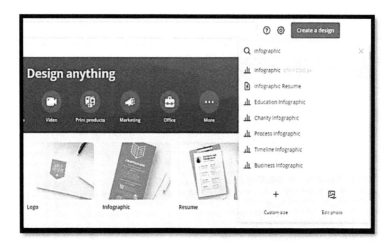

When you select "**Infographic**" from the search results, Canva will open a blank Canva document with a resolution of 800x2000 pixels by default. You can make your own infographic from scratch if you want to, but we'll be using a template that's already been made.

3. **Browse Through Infographic Templates**

There are several infographic templates on the left side of the screen after you start the dashboard. These are different in style, color, theme, and other ways.

In the search bar, you can type in buzzwords to quickly find the template type you need. Instead, scroll down until you find a template that works for your message. Then, click on it to make it editable. As soon as you start making changes to the template, you can quickly add a chart to show the data.

4. **Customize the Background**

You can either keep the background that came with the template or change it to fit your needs. Click on **Background** in the menu on the left to change the background. Then, pick a pattern or color that fits with your name or your own style.

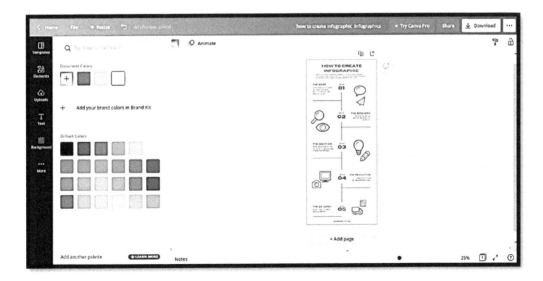

Once you've picked a background, use the editing menu right above the page to change how it looks. From the same menu, you can also change its color, add effects, change how transparent it is, and do other things.

5. Change the Text

To add your own text to the test text, click on it and press the "**Delete**" key to get rid of it. Then, write right into the text box, which is now empty.

To change the font, select the word you want to change and then use the text toolbar at the top of the screen to pick a font type, size, or color. You can also hit the **Text** button on the left side of the screen and then drag and drop the fancy font you want to use on the infographic. You can then change the size and make other changes as you like.

6. Add Graphic Elements

Canva sorts design elements into groups like photos, videos, grids, frames, charts, and lines and shapes. Click on a category and then drag and drop the part you want to use into the infographic.

Use the search tool to narrow down the results and find the exact picture you want. You can post your own graphics or photos to Canva and add them to the design. You can change the size of files and move them around the template too. Do not forget that some parts cost money to use. Things that cost money will have a crown icon in the bottom right corner.

How to Add a Chart to Your Infographic

You may need a chart to show your info at times. To add a chart to your slideshow, follow these steps:

1. Open a chart template. Then, find the "**More**" tab on the left sidebar and click on "**Charts**." There will be a number of charts for you to choose from.

2. Pick out a chart. We'll use a pie chart for this help.
3. The Edit tab is at the top of the page. Click it to change the image. In the left sidebar, a table with names and numbers will show up.

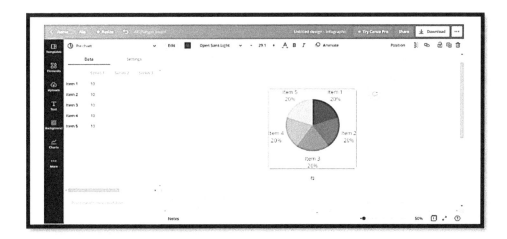

4. To enter your information, click on the boxes in the table. Click on the bottom row of the table to add more rows.

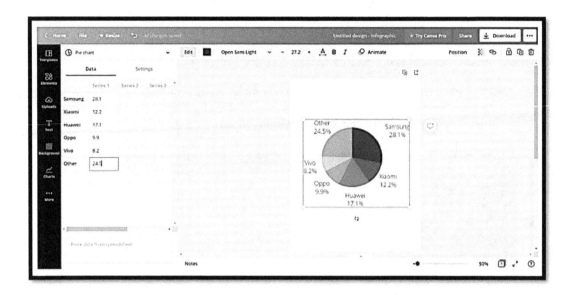

5. Click the **color tile** on the menu at the top of the screen to change the colors of the chart. Then, pick the color you want to use to change the chart's color style.

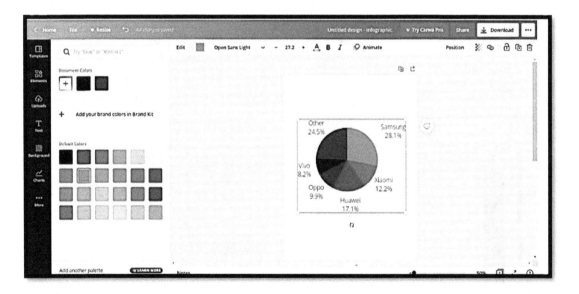

6. **Save and share your infographic.**
Once you're happy with how the chart looks, click the **three dots** in the upper right corner to see the **Share** button. You can share the infographic straight on social media sites or add it to your website.

You can save it as a PNG, JPG, or PDF file by clicking on the Download icon next to Print Infographics.

Use Canva to Create Infographics for Every Need

Infographics are a simple way to show the results of a poll or just teach someone something. Canva makes it much easier to make infographics, even for people who aren't artists. You can also make different kinds of infographics with it, so you're not stuck with just one style.

Designing Presentations

You can make presentations as easily with Canva as with Google Slides because it is a template design site where you can make beautiful papers. **Canva presentation design instructions are provided below.**
Step 1: Launch Canva
Under **Create a Design**, click **Presentation**.

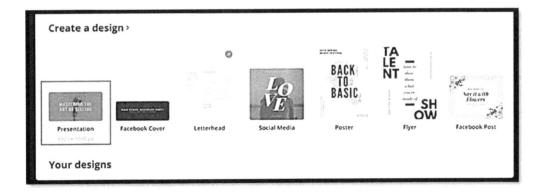

You can also use the search bar next to the words "**Design anything**" to look for "**Presentation**." You'll be taken to a blank area after clicking on **Presentation**. As with all of Canva's workspaces, there is a list of ready-made templates on the left. But if you need to make this show for work and don't have much time, it might be better to use a template. Canva sorts these templates into groups based on what they're supposed to be used for, from artistic projects to pitch decks. To begin this lesson, let's go to the **Professional Presentation** area, which has templates that are perfect for what we need. Pick the one you like.

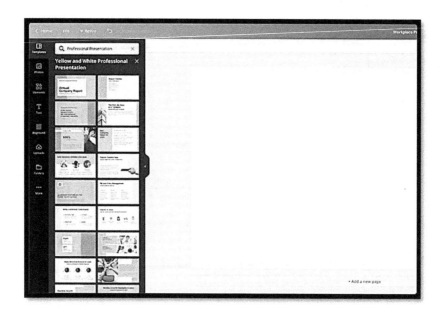

When you click on a design, a bunch of different pages will show up on the right. It's a little different on each of these pages, but they all use the same colors and features.

Step 2: Pick a Page Design, Change Your Text

One great thing about Canva is that these pages don't have to be put together in a certain way. You can use one or more designs more than once, right after each other, or never at all. To add a design to your first page, all you have to do is click on the blank workspace to make the page live. Then click on one of the designs that are already there on the left. Canva will load it into the page for you, and you can start making changes. I made the choice to use a design that would look good as a title page for this lesson. By clicking on each text box on this page, I can get rid of the empty text and write my own. You can make more changes to the size, color, weight, and space in the **Text** editing box, which is shown here in red.

Step 3: Adjust Your Visual Elements

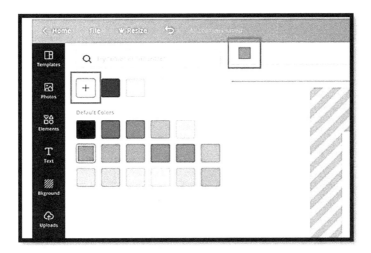

One of the most important things to think about when putting together your show is having the right text and not too much text. It's also very important to make sure that the visual parts fit up. You can keep or get rid of as many graphic features as you want in Canva. You can also move them around.

- To **Delete** an element, click on it so its bounding box shows up. Press **Delete**.
- To **Move** an element, click and drag it around the page.

The color swatch icon is at the top of the screen. Click on it to change the color of something. You can choose a color swatch from the palette that's already there, or click on the plus sign to bring up the color picker and pick your own color.

Step 4: Add Page Notes

Your show notes should be one of the last things you add to your page. You don't have to take notes, but they can help you remember what you want to say, especially if you're giving a speech in front of a group.

In Canva, go to the top right part of your page and click on the red "**Add notes**" icon. After you do that, another box will pop up. Fill in the box with your thoughts. Of course, you can't go over the word limit, but we don't think you will. Click **Save** when you're done.

Step 5: Add a New Page

Showing off a bunch of pages is what slideshows are all about. Of course, if you only had one page, it would be a poster, so you'll probably want to add more. Click on **+Add a new page** at the bottom of your area when you're done with the first page. There will be an extra page in your show thanks to Canva.

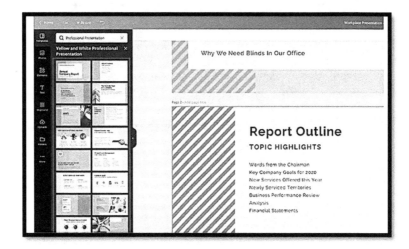

The page designs are on the left side of your screen. Click on them to change the style of this page. Pick the one you want and click on it.

If you're making more than one page, you might want to name them to keep your workspace neat. Look for the dotted line in the upper left area of your current page. This is where you can add labels to your pages. Type something when you click on it. You can add a new title from there.

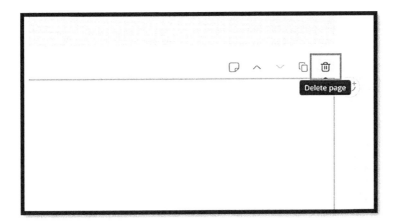

You can get rid of this whole new page if you don't like it at all. There is a trash can icon in the upper right part of the page. Press on it. Did you press "Delete" by mistake, or have you changed your mind? Don't worry—all you have to do is click the "**Undo**" button in the upper left area of your screen.

Step 6: Add a Graph

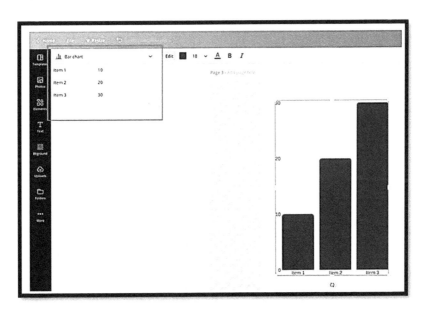

One of the best things about Canva is how easy it is to add graphs to your presentation. After that, you can change those graphs to fit your wants. Find a page design that already has a graph on it. After adding that page to your show, double-click on the graph on that page to make its box light up. The settings for your graph will show up in the toolbar on the left end. There is a dropdown menu at the top of those settings that tells you what kind of graph you are using. Below that is a list of things and how much they are worth. To change the names of these things, click on each box and begin typing. To change the numbers, click on the box and type in the new amount. Whenever you change these numbers, Canva will show you the new graph right away, so you can see how it looks.

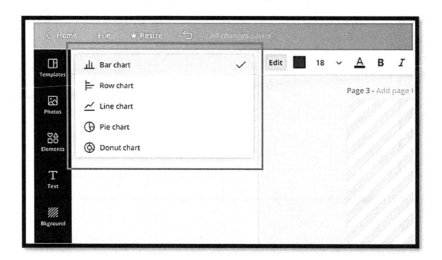

When you want to change the graph's style, you can click on the dropdown menu and pick a different one. The way your graph looks will be changed automatically by Canva, but the numbers will stay the same.

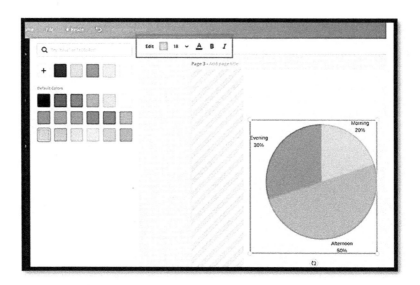

And finally, you can change the graph's color. First, make sure that the box around your graph is selected. Then, find the **Edit** controls in the upper left area of your screen. You should try them out to see what works best.

Step 7: Check Your Presentation and Add Transitions

As you finish, you should look over your talk for mistakes. You might also want to make the pages flow together better. In the upper right area of your screen, click the "**Present**" button to add smooth changes. Pick up the picture.

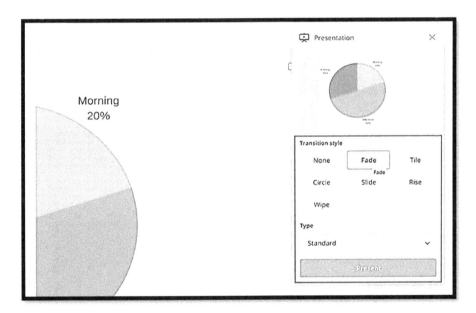

Canva will show you a drop-down menu where you can choose the **Transition style** you want when you click on that button. You can pick your **Type** after picking your **Transition style**. You can change the speed at which your show plays with Type.Once everything is set, click the blue "**Present**" button to see your slideshow play. When you click on it, it will open in full screen so you can look for mistakes. f you find any mistakes in your presentation, press the **Escape** key to close the window. Make any changes you think are necessary and then finish the design.

Step 8: Download Your Presentation for Work

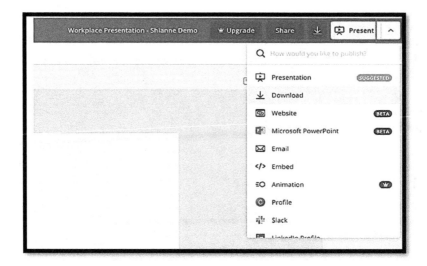

You are ready to download when your talk is over. Click on the dropdown menu next to the "**Present**" button to save your presentation or use it in a different manner. With a basic account, you can use most of these choices for free. The ones that aren't will have a gold "crown" next to them. Also, you have a lot of choices, such as saving the file, sending it to coworkers via email, or publishing it on another site. And that's it. You're done.

Ace That Slideshow Presentation

You can start looking around now that you know how to use Canva to make a presentation for work. You can change a lot of things, so it's best to play around with the settings yourself.

Create a Resume Using Canva

Making a resume takes a lot of time, but it's very important, especially if you're starting from scratch. There are online design tools that can help you make the right resume for the job, which is good news.

Creating a Resume on Canva from Scratch

How to use Canva to make a resume

1. **Start With a New Page**

If you want to make a resume, go to Canva's home page and click on **Create a Design**. The search will bring up different kinds of resumes. When you click on **Resume**, make sure the size is 8.5 x 11 inches.

2. **Change the Background**

On the Editor page of Canva, blank designs begin with a white page. Right-click on the background and choose "**Background Color.**" This will change the color. You can then choose a color from the list that turns up.

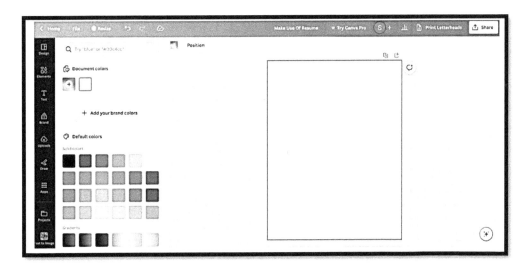

You can also click the plus sign (+) to open the **Color Picker** and see even more choices.

3. **Choose Your Elements**

After that, go to the **Elements** tab and look for the shapes and images. Keep in mind that elements with a crown on them cost money because they come with the Canva Pro membership. A simple shape is always a good way to draw attention to your resume. We'll choose one to use in the upper right part of ours. Go to **Elements > Shapes > See All** to find these shapes. Pick a form that you think will make your resume stand out.

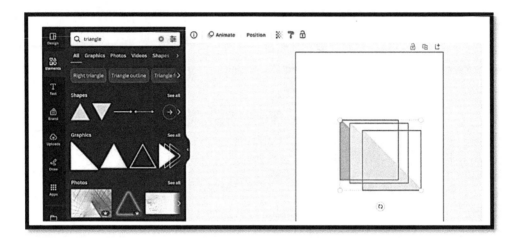

You can always type a shape name into the search bar if you can't find one you like. There will be Shapes, Graphics, Photos, and more where the shape will show up. If you need to, make sure to change the size. You don't want something too big that takes over the design. You can use the color picker in the upper left part of your workspace to change the color. The next step will show you how the shape is put together.

4. **Add Your Header**

Next, click on the **Text** tab when you're done adding Items. You'll see a number of different methods for adding text to your resume. Canva lets you make different kinds of papers with headings and subheadings. You can also choose to add a heading, a subheading, or text to the body on its own. You can see that a heading/subheading pair is too big for the header if you click on it. It will also be in the wrong place. To fix this, click on one of the text box's reference points and move it inward. Place your mouse over the text box, click and hold, and then move the box to where you want it.

131

You may see pink lines appear in different places when you move the text box. Your writing should line up with the shapes on the page. These pink lines are hints. If you want to change the alignment of your text from center to left-justified, click on the **Alignment** button. This will bring up a menu with all of your choices.

You don't have to highlight the text to change the style; just click on it. Then, in the upper left area, click on the font drop-down menu. Choose a font from the ones that are shown. Click inside the box and start typing to change the text.

5. **Add Your Professional Profile**

If you want to improve your resume, you should have a business profile. One to two sentences should do it. This is your chance to show why you're great and why they should hire you. In the **Text** tab, click **Add a Subheading** to add your own. Change the title to "Professional Profile" or something else that makes sense for your business. The text box should go on the page under the heading. Pick a clear style and place it there.

Next, click on **Add a little bit of body text**. You can fill out your bio in the new text box that comes up after clicking this. After you're done, put it under the heading "Professional Profile."

6. **Add a Divider**

You could add a graphic to the end of your resume, after your professional description, to make it stand out from the rest of it. Choose a line from the list of shapes and lines in **Elements > Shapes > Lines.** As long as it's easy and doesn't get in the way, it should not draw attention away from the top of the page. Move it around and change the color and size as needed.

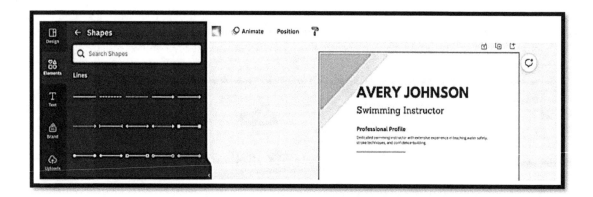

7. Fill Out Your Sections

Next, you need to fill out the different parts of your resume. List your personal information, what you've done, where you've worked, and what you've learned. On your resume, don't put anything that you don't need. To add the text boxes, do the same thing you did in the last step to make the text.

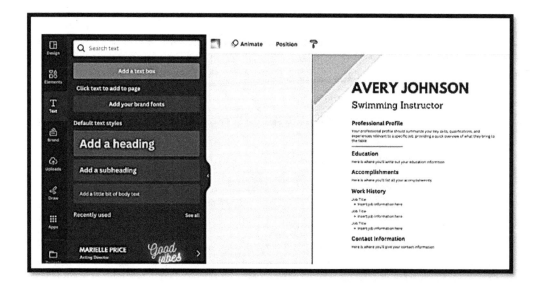

Copying the subheading and body text from the professional profile is an easy way to make sure that all of your sections have the same layout. Just change the text inside the box after you've copied it.

8. Add Links or Other Visual Interest

Your resume should be simple most of the time so it's easy to read. There are times, though, when adding pictures to your online resume can make it look better. Adding a few relevant links, like to your portfolio, previous articles, personal website, etc., can be very helpful if you don't have any relevant visuals.

It's easy to add a link to your resume in Canva. Once you've added the information you want to the "Links" part and clicked on the words you want the link to go to, it will be attached. If you select the text box, a three-dot icon will show up too. Pick **Link** from the three dots, type in the URL, and press **Enter**.

9. **Revise Your Resume and Group the Elements**

Always check to see if there is any spelling or language mistakes. If you learn how to proofread your resume, you'll make sure it looks expert. "Grouping" means that different parts of your page will be read together. These words mean that you can change each part separately in Canva, but you can move the parts as a single unit across the page. This helps if you want to change the design but keep the order of the different parts.

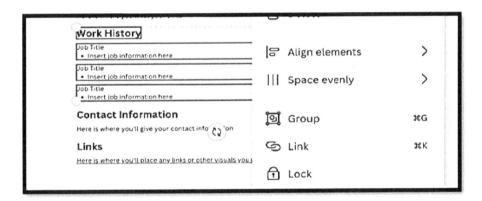

To put things into a group, click and drag over the things you want to group until purple lines appear around them. Click on **Group** once they are all chosen. Make any last changes you want to your resume's look, and you're done.

Creating a Resume on Canva Using a Template

There are times when people don't have the time or desire to make a professional resume from scratch. If that sounds like you, you should use one of Canva's resume templates to make one.

1. **Select a Template**

Utilizing a resume template is a very simple process compared to making one from scratch. Type "**Resume**" into the search bar on the home page of Canva and press "**Enter**." The next page will have thousands of resume templates to choose from—some even come with a cover letter template. Select one that you think will work for you and click **Customize This Template**.

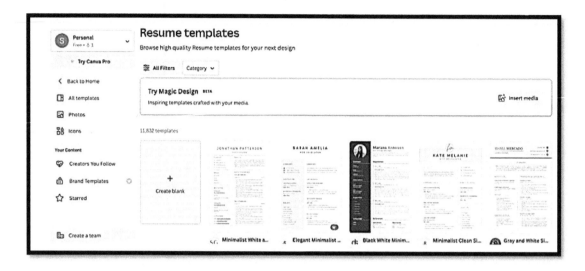

2. **Fill Out the Template With Your Information**

In each template, there are different parts that you need to fill out. If you click on the text box, you can make changes as you go, just like when you're making a resume from start.

It is possible to delete or move parts of the resume if you decide that they don't fit the style of resume you want to make. Remember that all of the templates can be changed in any way you want.

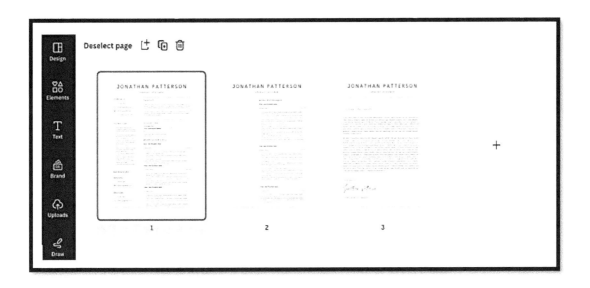

It's easier to move a whole area when it's already grouped, even if it's just to a different page. To learn how to group a part, go to step nine above.

CHAPTER 9
CANVA FOR BUSINESS

Creating Logos

Step 1: Login and Search for a Template
You can use the search bar on the homepage or click on "logo" under the "You might want to try..." choices to find Canva's huge library of ready-made logo templates after logging into your account.

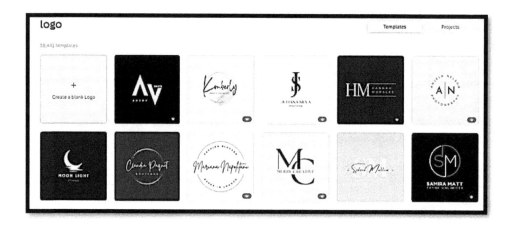

This shows the huge library of Canva templates. You can scroll through it and look at every design, but since there are more than 50,000 of them, you might want to use the filters to save some time. With these choices, you can narrow down your options based on the theme, style, topic, or features you like best.

Take the case of opening a bakery as an example. If so, you can use the filters to see only the more than 1,000 logos that fit the "bakery" theme. You can then narrow it down even more by picking a style, like simple or modern until you find a logo design you like.

You could also pick "modern" as your style and "computer" as your theme if you wanted your new computer repair business to look bold and up-to-date. We should let you know that if you see a template with a small crown icon, you can only use it if you purchase Canva Pro. Although it does cost $12 a month, you can get all of the Pro-only templates and files for free for 30 days if you're still not sure if the platform is right for you. You can use the filters to find the right template for the type of logo you want to make. Then, click on it to open it in the Canva design tool.

Step 2: Choose Graphic and Design Elements

We chose to pretend that we are starting a new travel service and need a logo for it for this lesson. The first thing we need to do after opening our favorite logo in the Canva editor is to add any images or other things we want to use.

For this, click on the images you don't want and tap the trash can icon to get rid of them.

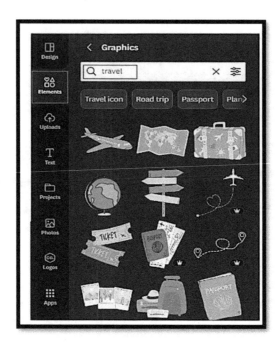

Next, go to the Canva menu and select Elements > Drawings. Then, use the search function to find the drawings that are right for your business. We looked for "travel" in this case.

- If you click on an image, it will be added to your logo.

After that, you can change it in many ways, such as:
- Using the four dots on the corner to resize it
- Using the position feature to rearrange the order of different elements
- Use your cursor to drag the element around your design and place it where you want it.

Do this again and again until you're ready for the next step. You can add as many images, lines, shapes, or other elements as you want.

Step 3: Choose Your Colors and Fonts

You can always change the colors of your image if you like the way it looks but don't think it fits with your brand. To change the color of your images, borders, or other parts, click on them. This will bring up the color boxes in the upper right corner of your editing menu. These boxes are the same color as your part, which you can see.

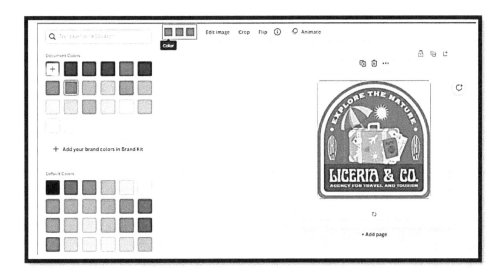

If you tap those boxes, the color choices will show up. Canva is smart to show you a list of colors that were already used in your design.

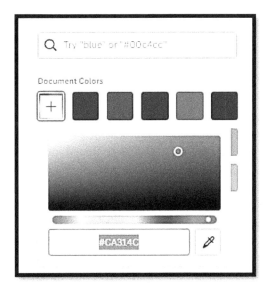

You can also choose from a list of pre-set colors. To get the exact color you want, click the plus sign with the rainbow edge, use the sliders, or type in the hex code.

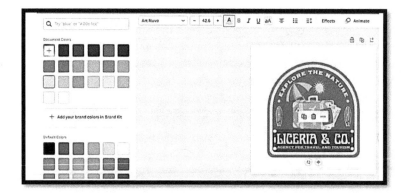

- To change the color of some text, pick it and click the "A" icon with a line through it.
- This will show the same color choices as the picture above.

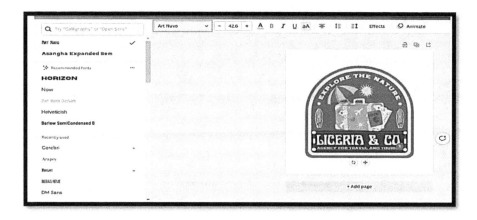

To change the font, click on the word you want to change. This will bring up a menu with different fonts for you to choose from.

You can also go to the text menu and add some beautiful font choices that have already been put together with your design.

Step 4: Add Your Text

- The last thing you need to do is change the usual text to your business name.
- It's very simple to do that.
- To add the name of your small business, just select the text and highlight it. Then type it in like you would in Microsoft Office®.

Step 5: Download Your New Logo

After you've done all of that, you can make any last changes you want to your design until you're happy with the end logo.

After that, you should get that image and use it. To do that, press "Share" and then "Download." This will bring up a list of file types that you can use to save the file.

Designing Social Media Graphics

1. **Choose the Right Dimensions for Each Platform**

Images need to be a certain size for each social media site. From Canva's built-in choices, it's easy to choose the right size, so your designs will look great on all devices.

Tip: Start by clicking on *Create a Design* and selecting from options like **Instagram Post (1080 x 1080 px)**, **Facebook Cover (820 x 312 px)**, or **LinkedIn Banner (1584 x 396 px)**.

2. **Start with a Template, but Customize It**

Canva has a huge selection of templates that are specially designed for various social media sites. That being said, templates are great places to start, but you should change them to make your brand stand out.

Tip: Choose a template that matches the style and tone of your brand, and then modify the colors, fonts, and images to align with your branding.

3. **Incorporate Your Brand's Colors and Fonts**

Using the same colors and fonts over and over again helps build a brand's personality. Use the Brand Kit tool in Canva Pro to save your brand's color scheme, fonts, and logo so they are easy to find.

Tip: Use the **Color Picker Tool** to match the exact colors of your brand, and stick to no more than 2-3 fonts to maintain a clean look.

4. Utilize Grids and Alignment Tools for Balance

For images to look professional, they need to be aligned and spaced correctly. You can structure your design with Canva's Grids and Guides to make sure that everything is lined up and spaced out properly.

Tip: Enable **Rulers and Guides** (found under *File > View*) to position elements precisely, and use the **Position Tool** to center objects or distribute them evenly.

5. Choose High-Quality Images and Illustrations

There are a lot of pictures and drawings in Canva's library, but it's important to pick high-quality ones that fit your message.

Tip: Use keywords like "minimal," "modern," or "bold" in the **Photos** tab to find images that match your style. Always double-check the resolution and quality before adding them to your design.

6. Add Text Overlays for Impactful Messaging

One great way to make your message stand out is to add text backgrounds. For headers, use clear, bold fonts, and for context, you might want to pair them with smaller subheadings.

Tip: Use **Text Effects** like *Shadow* or *Lift* to make your text pop, and experiment with **Transparency** settings for a layered look.

7. Use Icons and Shapes to Enhance Visual Appeal

Use shapes and icons to draw attention to important parts of text or break it up. There are many icons and shapes in Canva's library that can be changed in size, color, and order.

Tip: Search for **"Social Media Icons"** or **"Arrow Shapes"** to find visual elements that guide the viewer's eye through your design.

8. Leverage Canva's Filters and Effects for Cohesive Style

Effects and filters can change the whole mood of your design. You can make all of your drawings look the same by using Canva's built-in filters.

Tip: Click on your image, go to **Filters**, and experiment with options like *Retro*, *Grayscale*, or *Dramatic*. Adjust the intensity for subtle enhancements.

9. Create Reusable Templates for Consistency

If you post a lot on social media, making templates that you can use again and again will save you time and help you stay consistent.

Tip: Design a few core templates for different types of posts (e.g., quotes, promotions, or announcements), and save them in your Canva folder. Just swap out the text and images as needed.

10. Export in the Right Format

For social media, make sure your graphics are exported in the best style so they look clear and professional:

- **PNG**: Best for images with transparent backgrounds or high-quality visuals.
- **JPEG**: Ideal for photos and images with gradients.
- **MP4**: Use for short video clips or animated posts.

Tip: Always check the file size and resolution to ensure fast loading times on social media platforms.

CHAPTER 10

CANVA TEMPLATES AND CUSTOMIZATION

Modifying Pre-Designed Templates

Finding the Right Template

Selecting a template that fits your needs is the first step in changing a pre-designed design. When designing an Instagram post, for instance, you can use keywords like "Instagram post," "holiday sale," or "motivational quotes" to find templates. Canva also lets you sort templates by certain dimensions, themes, or groups. This function keeps you from having to start from scratch, which saves time. You can open a template right in the Canva editor after choosing it. This is the magic spot for customizing.

Customizing the Text

Changing the text is one of the easiest and most useful ways to change a template. The templates on Canva have sample text that you can change to see how the style will look with real text. You just need to click on the text boxes and type your own words where the sample text is. You can put in details about an event, business names, quotes, or anything else that fits with your design. You can change the text in Canva by changing its font, size, color, alignment, and space, as well as replacing it. Canva has a large font library with everything from fancy styles to big display fonts. You can share your own fonts or use fonts that match your brand if you're working on a brand project. To change the text, just drag and resize the text boxes to make them fit better in the plan. You can even make the text stand out by adding shadows, outlines, or background colors.

Changing Colors

Colors are an important part of making your design look good. It's easy to change the colors of text, backgrounds, and other design features in Canva. You can use specific hex codes to keep things consistent if you're working with a brand theme. You can also play around with the color wheel to find colors that go well together. You can choose from more than one tone of color. You have a lot of artistic freedom with Canva because you can add gradients, transparency effects, or textured backgrounds. If the template you choose comes with a color scheme that you don't like, you can change it all by clicking "**Change All**." This changes everything in the template immediately to match the new color scheme you picked.

Editing Images

Templates often have pictures or drawings that you can use as placeholders to show how your design might look. You can change these pictures to your own or look through Canva's huge collection of free and paid stock photos. There are two easy ways to add your own photos: drag and drop them into the Canva editor, or click the "**Upload**" button. You can change the images to fit the template's placeholders after you've put them. You can crop, resize, and move pictures around in Canva's editing tools. For a more unique touch, you can also add overlays, use filters, and change the brightness, contrast, and saturation. Canva has effects, like duotones and pixelation, that you can use to change the way your pictures look and give them a unique look.

Rearranging Layouts

Canva templates can be changed in any way you want, so you're not limited to the style that came with the template. You can change the parts as needed if you think some are too crowded or if you want to draw attention to a certain part of the design. With a simple drag-and-drop move, you can resize, spin, or move things like text boxes, images, and icons. If you want to add more parts, you can do so without any problems with Canva. To improve the design, for example, you can add more text, icons, or decorative shapes. On the other hand, if you think a template has too many parts, you can get rid of the ones you don't need to make the design simpler.

Using Canva's Built-in Features

Canva also has more complicated tools that you can use to make your changes even more accurate. As an example:
- **Grid and Snap Features:** The Grid and Snap features help you line up elements correctly, which makes for a clean and professional layout.
- **Layering:** You can change how elements are arranged in Canva by moving them forward or backward. This gives your design depth.
- **Group and Ungroup:** This feature lets you change several things at once or separate them so you can make individual changes.

Incorporating Graphics and Icons

You can use any of the thousands of free and paid graphics and icons in Canva's library in your design. You can search for these images and change their size, color, and placement so they fit perfectly in your template. If you're making a business flyer, for example, you can add items like a phone or a location marker to make it more useful.

Finalizing Your Design

Once you're happy with the changes you've made, Canva gives you a number of ways to finish your design. It can be downloaded in different types of files, like PNG, JPG, or PDF. If you're making a movie or animation, you can save it as an MP4. You don't have to leave Canva to share your design on social media or email it to someone; you can do that right from the app.

Create and Publish a Template in Canva

It will be easy for you to make your own templates if you know how to use Canva to make designs. From design to making a template, there are only a few more steps.

Step 1: Subscribe to Canva Pro

You need a Canva Pro account to design something or make a template that you can use again. You can design a template in the same way as any other Canva design workflow, but only Canva Pro users can save it as a template. After making your Canva Pro account, you'll need to log in.

Step 2: Create a Design

On Canva's home page, go to the top right corner and click on **Create a Design**. From the small dropdown menu, you can choose one of the common social media sizes. If you know the exact size of your project, you can also choose **Custom Size** at the bottom and type in your own measurements.

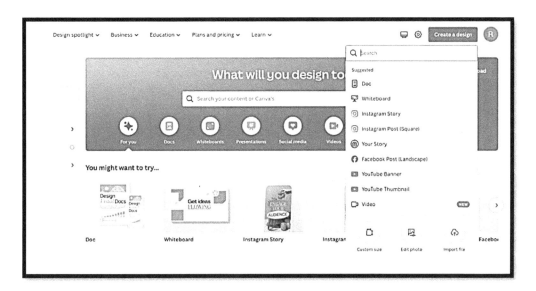

You can also use the search bar in the menu to type in the type of media you want to design for. Then, pick the result from the list that comes up.

Step 3: Design Your Template

The editor in Canva lets you make your design in any way you like. Add pictures, writing, and a background. Set it up the way you want your template design to look. When you make a template that can be used for many things, you should think about how the style might change if new images or word lengths come out in the future.

Step 4: Publish Your Canva Template

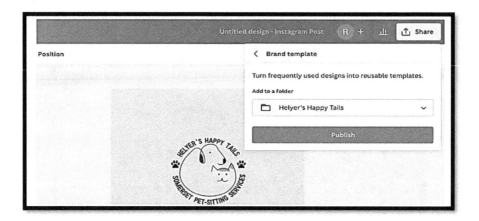

Select Share > Brand Template when you're done with your design. Here is where you can pick a folder to save your template. Then, click **Publish** or **Add** to save the template in the folder. When you save or post your template, a link is made that lets other people see your template design. To share, copy and paste the link.

Step 5: Open and Edit Your Saved Template

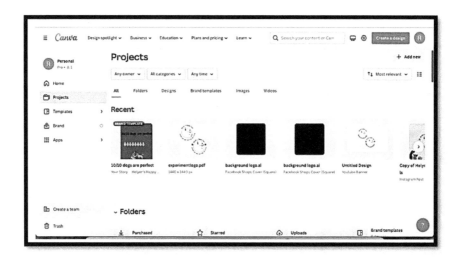

It's important to save your template so you can use it again. To get to it, go to the Canva home page and click on the menu on the left. On the Projects page, you can see your most recent projects. Below those, you'll see where you saved your templates. Find a template and click on it to open it in the editing box. You can change what you need to in the template and then save it like any other Canva project. Then you can use it however you like.

How to Create and Publish a Canva Template on a Phone or Tablet

You can get most of the same Canva tools on your phone or tablet as you can on your computer. In a few similar steps, you can make Canva templates on your phone or tablet.

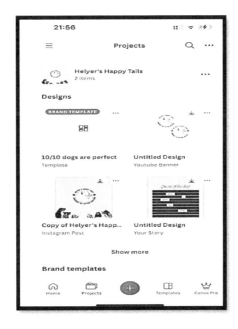

1. Sign in to Your Canva Pro Account.
2. Tap **+** to start a new design.
3. Make your design.
4. Go to **Share** > **Brand Template** and choose a folder.
5. Tap **Projects** to find your saved templates.

Can You Import a Premade Template in Canva?

You can bring in PDF, AI, and PSD files that were made somewhere else. You can't change individual parts in Canva when you import PSD or AI files, though, so these can't be used for editable Canva templates. There is good news: Canva lets you change PDFs. This means you can save your designs made in Photoshop, Illustrator, or InDesign as PDFs and use them as templates. You can import individual parts that you've made elsewhere to make templates in Canva instead of PSDs or other formats that you can't change. You can use Canva's template-making feature by adding all of your own design elements. Your template designs will be different from those made by other Canva users who use Canva's given elements.

Simplify Your Workflow with Canva Templates

Using ready-made template designs for a range of reasons is what Canva does for a living. You can start from scratch when you use Canva, but making your own template makes starting from scratch easier when you need to make a lot of designs that are all the same. You can save time in the future by using Canva Pro to make templates. Your designs can even make you money if someone buys them and doesn't want to make their own.

CHAPTER 11

CANVA APP AND CANVA PRO

Navigating the Canva App

The app's main area is made up of four screens: Home, Projects, Templates, and Canva Pro. Allow us to go over each part and what it holds.

The Home Screen

We'll start with **Home**, which is the first thing you see when you log in and open the app. It looks like most social apps, so it's pretty simple to use. At the top of the screen is the **menu button**. It lets you do some of the same things as the tabs, like open **Projects and Templates**. As a Pro member, you can only get **Content Planner and Brand Hub.** However, you can also connect more advanced tools and apps with Canva, like **Smartmokups**. There is a **search bar** next to the choices. Keywords can help you find projects or templates that you have already finished. Below that, there are tabs that let you see the thousands of templates that come with the software. **"For You"** will be different each time you open the app, like how Spotify does, based on how you use Canva. Most of the time, it will show you your most recent projects, different design sizes, and templates that you might be interested in. Each one will be clearly labeled with what it's for. You can start working on different kinds of templates in other tabs, like ones for **social media, videos, presentations, prints,** and more. The page will change to show you everything you can do about that subject if you click on any of them.

From the home screen, you can start making a new picture in a number of ways. When you click on a template you like, a new window will appear where you can begin making changes. To make a design, click on the type of design you want, such as **Instagram Post or Mobile Video**. You can pick a template or start from scratch on this page. Also, press the **purple plus (+)** sign at the bottom of the screen to start over. You can choose the size (Custom or something like Facebook Post) when you tap it. After that, a new, empty space will appear.

The Projects Screen

You can see all the things you've made on your computer, phone, or account on the Projects screen. You can see the files, photos, and thoughts you store in the cloud. In the upper right part of each drawing picture are two buttons. The arrow icon lets you download the picture and the three dots icon brings up a menu with many options, such as **Edit, Make a Copy,** and **Share**.

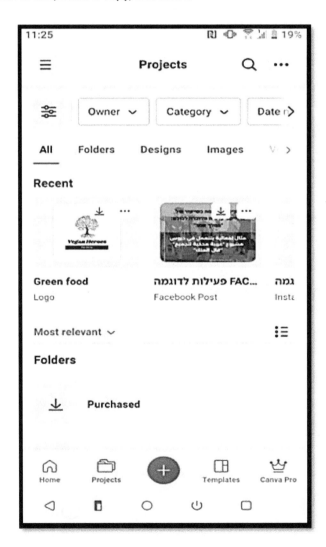

Remember that **Edit** will change the picture you had before. Instead, click "**Make a Copy**" if you like your design and want to keep it for later use.

The Templates Screen

It's kind of like the home screen, but this one is mostly about templates. You can look through each template or by subject with the buttons at the top. You can also look at what other Canva users have picked as a theme, such as Earth Day or Juneteenth. Holidays or times of the year are often to blame. You can find areas like **Features Collections, Trending Near You, New on Canva**, and more. All of them are meant to give you ideas.

The Canva Pro Screen

You can see the last shot if you pay for the service. This is where you'll find options like **Brand Kit, Premium Content**, and social media plans.

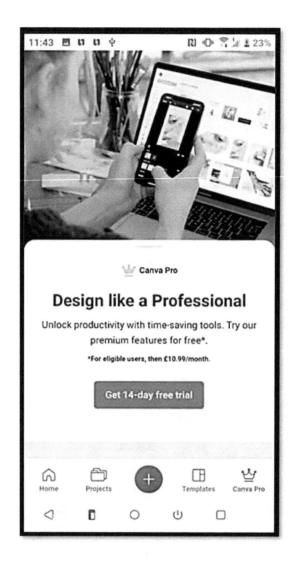

Create and Modify Your Design

Now let's talk about the picture-making tools you can use. To start, choose one of the templates. We used an Instagram post. Keep in mind that not all templates can be used with a free account. Try to find templates that don't say "Pro" or "Paid." This picture lets you change any part of it by clicking on the words, pictures, background, or shapes. You can also move it around, and the app will help you line up things in the middle or with other things in the shot. The **Undo and Redo** buttons are in the upper left corner. They look like two round lines pointing in different directions. If you don't like any of the changes you made, click them. When you tap on a different part of the screen, you get a different set of choices. They can be found in the bar at the bottom of the screen. There is a "**Replace**" button on this picture. If you press it, you can add a picture from your phone's gallery, take a picture with your camera, or pick one by Canva.

On top of that, you can crop the picture; add colors and effects make it move, and more. To change something, tap a text box once and then press **Edit**. You can change the style, size, layout, and other things after that. The **Nudge** tool makes a big difference. There is a one-pixel step between each direction button press. This works more accurately than a touch screen. You can also add new things to the design by pressing the plus (+) button. You can change the template (which will replace the current template), add sound and pictures, change the background, and get to all of your files from that page.

Download or Share Your Canva Design

It's time to use the picture (or movie) that you've changed everything about to make it perfect. To do that, press the buttons at the top of the screen. The down arrow saves the picture to your phone, and the up arrow lets you share it with other people. The Share button is great about the Canva app. When you're done with your picture, you can use WhatsApp or Slack to send it straight to work or friends. If you press the "**Share**" button, you can also post your picture straight to Instagram or TikTok. If you were on a PC, you would have to first move the picture to your phone. You can even set the post to go live on social media at a certain time if you have a Pro account.

Differences between Mobile and Desktop

Users can access the Canva app on both mobile and desktop devices thanks to its multipurpose design. In terms of basic functionality, both are the same, but the interface, usability, and features are very different. Knowing these differences can help you choose the best option for your needs or figure out how to improve your workflow when you switch between devices.

Desktop Version

You can use a web browser or a desktop app to get to Canva on a laptop. This version has more advanced tools and a bigger area, which makes it perfect for designs with lots of small details. You can see your project more clearly because the screen is bigger, so you can work on complicated plans or manage many things at once. The desktop version is easy to use because it has a toolbar and a sidebar that nicely organizes all the features. This makes it easy to get to tools like editing text, making changes to images, and adding layers. You can drag and drop items without any problems, and using a mouse or keyboard makes things more precise, especially when resizing, cropping, or aligning things. The PC version is also better for doing more than one thing at once. It's easy for users to start and switch between multiple tabs or projects. This is helpful for managing big campaigns or working on designs that need to look the same in all formats. The desktop's ability to work with outside tools is another benefit. It's easy to share files from your computer, you can speed up tasks with shortcuts, and you can even connect to third-party software to do things like exporting or importing data. Desktop Canva also has powerful collaboration tools that let teams work on projects together in real-time, with notes and shared access, as long as everyone has a stable internet connection, which is usually possible on desktop computers.

The Mobile Version

The app for smartphones and tablets lets you use the mobile version of Canva, which is designed to be portable and easy to use. It's designed for quick changes, creating on the go, or handling simpler, smaller projects. The interface is small and designed to work well with touch screens. With just a few taps, you can add parts, change layouts, or add text. When working on designs with a lot of layers or small features, though, the smaller screen size can be a problem. On mobile devices, scrolling and zooming happen more often, and some users may find it harder to stay precise without a mouse or keyboard. There are some things that the mobile app can't do that it can't do with Canva. When compared to the desktop, advanced tools like background remover, animation effects, or multi-page browsing might not work as smoothly or be as easy to use. Mobile devices may not have as much storage space or faster working power as desktops, which can make uploading files a bit of a pain, especially for bigger projects. The mobile app, on the other hand, is great because it lets you quickly share or download designs directly to social media sites, email, or chat apps. This makes it a good choice for social media managers or users who need results right away.

Performance

Desktop computers usually process things faster, especially when working on projects with lots of layers, high-resolution pictures, or animation effects. Mobile devices, on the other hand, depend a lot on how fast the internet is and what the gadget can do. Tablets are good for people who need to work away from their desks but don't want to carry around a smartphone. They are small and light but have bigger screens than smartphones.

Canva Pro Features

Overview of Canva Pro

You can subscribe to Canva Pro either once a month or once a year to use it. The new Canva is better than the old one. For professional designers, it has a lot of features and functions that are made to meet their wants. For those who sign up for Canva Pro, there is a huge library of templates that can be used for many things, such as social media posts, slideshows, posters, and more. There is also a huge library of high-quality photos, videos, and music tracks that users can use to improve the look of their designs. Canva Pro is great because it has many tools that can help you get work done. Magic Resize is one of these. It lets people quickly change designs to fit different sizes without having to start from scratch. The Brand Kit tool lets users build and manage their brand's visual identity by putting all of their logos, colors, and fonts in one place. With Canva Pro, users can make changes to files and share them in real-time. This makes it great for groups working on projects together. Folders make it easy for users to organize their drawings, and Canva's cloud storage gives them unlimited room.

Features Exclusive to Canva Pro

- **Magic Resize**: This feature lets users easily change the size of designs to fit different screen sizes. It saves time and work because layouts don't have to be changed for each device.
- **Brand Kit**: Users can make their brand's style clear in all designs by using their own fonts, colors, and logos. With this feature, graphic branding is always done in a regular and professional way.
- **Background Remover**: This tool makes it easier to change photos by letting you get rid of backgrounds with just one click. You can use this feature to make layouts that look clean and professional.
- **Premium Templates**: You can get access to a huge library of well-designed templates for a wide range of projects, such as ads, presentations, social media images, and more. These templates give you a strong base for quickly making content that looks good.
- **Collaboration Tools**: Canva Pro lets team members work together easily by letting them change and share files in real time. People can comment on each other's work and share their thoughts. This makes the work go faster.
- **Animation**: Animations give designs movement and interaction, which makes them more interesting for people to look at. This tool lets you make live presentations, social media posts, and other kinds of multimedia content.
- **Unlimited Folders and Storage**: You can quickly order your drawings with unlimited folders, and you can keep your files safe in Canva's cloud storage. This makes sure that users can do their jobs well and access their work from anywhere.
- **Priority Support**: You'll be able to get in touch with Canva's support team faster. They're available 24 hours a day, 7 days a week to help with any technology issues or questions. This makes sure that people who need help get it quickly.

Using Canva Pro Tools

Magic Resize

This is a helpful tool called Canva Magic Resize. It lets you quickly and easily changes the size of your designs for different platforms, so you don't have to start from scratch. This lets you make a set of pictures that all of your sites will use and they will all look the same. **This is the way to do it.**

1. Start with a blank design and make a picture that will sell your brand.
2. When you're happy with the difference, click the "**Resize**" button in the top left corner of your screen.
3. After that, you'll see a drop-down button that lets you change the size of your picture for different social media sites. You can also make a post in any size you want with the "custom size" option.
4. Click the "**Create**" button next to the platform(s) whose size you want to change. Canva will open a new tab every time you change the size of an item.
5. Since the posts won't be changed exactly, you'll need to make changes to each one to get the best look. You will save a lot of time and make sure your business stays the same.
6. You can save or share your pictures right from Canva when you're done with them.

Creating your brand kit with Pro

The brand kit is in your Canva profile. In the left bar, there is a link that says "Brand." This will take you to the page with the image. In the top right corner of this page, there is an "**Add new**" button that you can use to make a new kit or go to an existing one. **Here are two brand kits that I put together:**

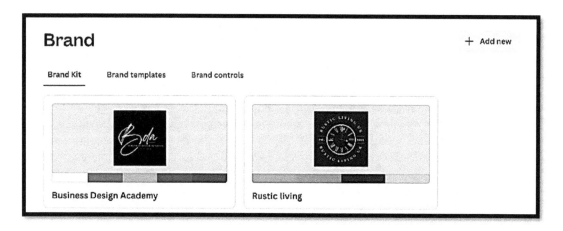

We can make a new kit by clicking "**Add new**" and then "**Brand Kit**." This is also where you can make brand templates that you can save and use again, which will help you stay on brand:

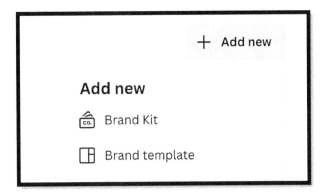

Right now, it's not important to change the name of your kit. After that, click Make. We now have a kit that is empty and ready to be filled:

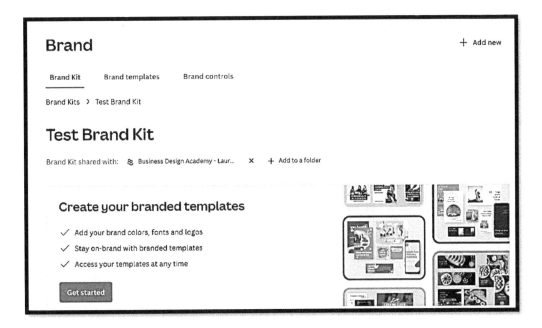

From the "**Get Started**" button, you can go to "**Quick Create**" and make your first set of named templates. Let's add our picture by going down to "logo." If you made your own, that's great, but if you're just starting out, a template is better. The logo must be in the form of a picture to be added. You will need to download your image if you haven't already. Click the **Share** button at the top of the image and choose **Download**. The format will be set to PNG for you. After that, save it to your phone or computer. To add our logo, we need to go back to the brand kit we made earlier and find it under "**Brand Logos.**" Click the plus sign to add it. It will now show up where the plus sign was. The brand kit now has your image in it. Now you can do the same thing with any other logos or sub-logos you have:

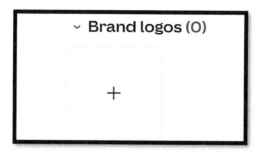

Now we'll add our brand colors. Did you make a note of your HEX numbers from the color list? You need them right now. I'm going to use the color scheme I made from a picture of a pink flower:

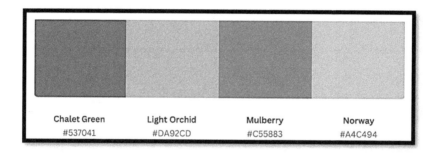

Chalet Green	Light Orchid	Mulberry	Norway
#537041	#DA92CD	#C55883	#A4C494

Click on the plus sign next to the Color palette to make a new color pattern. This means we can now add any color we want. Move the white circle around to change the color, or copy and paste your HEX code to get the exact color your brand needs. I copied and pasted all four of the hex numbers from my color scheme over. I did the same thing again and pressed the + sign to add each color. I've never seen this set of colors before.

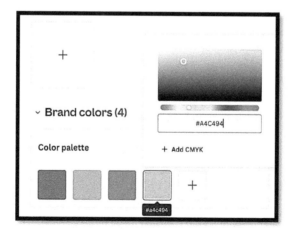

When you click the plus sign at the top of the color palette area, you can add as many as you want. You can add as many as you need, say if you need to use different colors for different jobs.

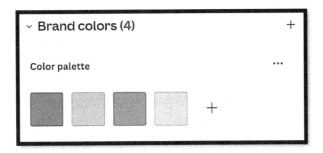

In this last part, we'll look at adding our fonts. These are the three places where you can add your title, subtitle, and body fonts. The Canva drop-down menu lets you choose your type. If you click on each one, you can:

Do the same thing for all three boxes to add your brand's fonts. What if you can't find the font you need? If you have a Pro account, you can add these fonts to Canva:

Before you can send the font, you will need to make sure it is the right file type. Most of the time, this is an OTF or TTF file. These will be sent to you when you buy or download the source font. Click on "**Upload a font**" after you find the file. After that, it will be put here so you can use it. It will also show up in the list of fonts when you are drawing.

Create Your Brand Kit with a Free Account

That's all there is to making a brand kit for Pro users. It's not possible for free users to get these choices. One thing you can do with the HEX numbers is add three colors to a palette. You can also use a Canva template to make your kit. Some search terms that will help you find templates are "**Moodboard**," "**Brandboard**," and "**Brand kit**." Choose the one that speaks to you, but keep in mind that you can change everything on it:

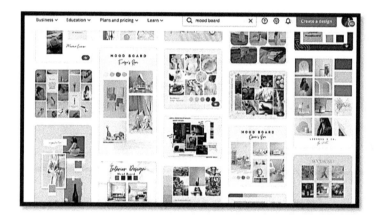

Pay close attention to both the moodboard and the brand board; they each have their own parts. Label templates for Brand Boards will also have font choices and sometimes sub mark spots:

This template is what I chose to show you how it looks:

This template has a number of different fonts, color rings, and picture blocks. To change any of the pictures, either add your own to Canva or use one of the ones that are already there and drag it into the empty space. It will take the place of any pictures that are already there. You can add your HEX numbers when you click on a color circle. You can also enter your HEX code if you click on the plus sign next to the color:

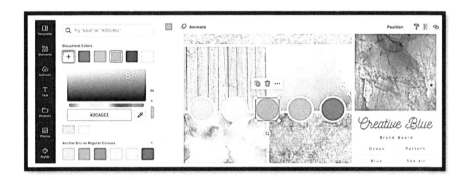

Last but not least, you can change the style to match your brand. Click on the text box and then use the drop-down menu to change the font. You can pick from a lot of free fonts. You can also change the text to the name of the font:

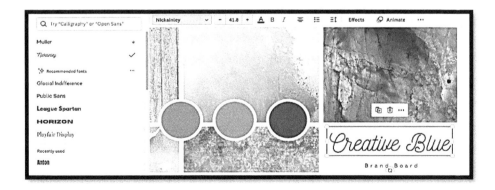

This is the coolest way to put together your brand kit. That you can print out and put up. As your business grows and your brand changes, you can make changes to the template and print it again. When you're making designs for your business, though, these options on the left won't show up. These will only be in your account if you have Pro and have set up the brand kit.

Content Planner

It's hard and important to make posts for social media that people will want to read. Making sure it goes live at the best time for your fans is just as important. It is now very easy to do this with Canva's Content Planner. That way, you can schedule your posts for the best times, days, and weeks ahead of time and keep track of how many views, clicks, likes, and comments they get. Make a plan for how you will use social media. This will help you do well on it.

Post Your Content in Fewer Clicks

You probably already know how to use Canva to make video and picture posts that look great on social media. In the past, you could download your pictures and then post them on a social networking site or a tool for making plans for the next day. This new habit will save you a lot of time because it lets you plan, organize, and even post your content right from Canva. When you use the content planner that comes with Canva, you can design, share, and look at stats all from the same place.

The Easy Way to Plan Social Content

You should know that the Content Planner comes with Canva Pro. When you become a Canva Pro member, you can get the Background Remover and the Magic Switch. People really like these two tools, and they save them a lot of time. Canva Pro is free to try for 30 days to see if you like everything it has to offer.

Every Plan Needs a Calendar

On the home page of Canva, click "**Content Planner**" to get to the calendar. Here is a list of what you're going to post on social media over the next few weeks. There are already a lot of well-known cyberdates from all over the world. Get ideas for posts and ways to share your voice in hashtags that might become famous and get a lot of attention. If you go to "**filters**" and uncheck the "**social media holidays**" box, these will go away. You'll start over after this. You can also add birthdays, holidays, and events that are important to your business in your area.

Schedule an Existing Design

Setting up times for things is very simple. In the Content Planner, find a date on your calendar and click the "**+**" sign. This is where you can see your most recent work, begin a new design from scratch, or use a template. To use a picture that has already been made, just click on it, choose the channel, and write a description. Set it to happen right away or save it as a draft to finish later. Your post can be changed or taken down at any time if you decide to.

Scheduling New Designs

Click "**new**" and then "**post**." There are a lot of templates to choose from, which makes it easier to write material. With the Magic Switch Tool (opens in a new tab or window), you can change their sizes so that they work on any machine. That's right, you can start over with a new picture. You can change the colors, add new text, and make the template your own in any way you like. After that, it's time to make plans. After that, all I have to do is click "share" and then "share on social." Choose where you want to post it. Last, give your post a title, change the date if needed, and either plan it or save it for later.

Background Remover

You can remove the backgrounds of up to 500 shots every 24 hours. Right now, Background Remover can only be used on pictures that are less than 9MB in size. There will be no background in any picture you share that is bigger than 10MP. It will be shrunk down to 10MP. You can get rid of the backgrounds on pictures you add to "**Project**" files. But you won't be able to use the Erase and Restore brushes. You can find out more about it on Canva Picture Maker.

To remove a background on a desktop computer in the Canva Editor, simply:
1. You can either upload your picture or pick one from our gallery.
2. On the top toolbar, click the "**Edit Image**" button.
3. Next, on the left-hand screen that comes up, choose "**Background Remover**."
4. After that, click "**Erase**" to get rid of the background.
5. The background will disappear like magic after you click "**Erase**."
6. When you're happy with how your picture looks without a background, click "**Apply**" to keep the changes. But you can also choose "**Restore**" to remove any changes.
7. Finally, all you have to do is drag your new picture into place.

To remove a background on your mobile in the Canva Editor, simply:
1. Click on the picture you want to change.
2. Select "**Effects**" from the list of tools below the editor.
3. Click on "**Background Remover**."
4. Wait for the background to be processed.

Using the Background Remover Tool on Your Videos

You can only remove backgrounds from movies that are less than 90 seconds long at the moment. If you edit a video in Canva, this tool won't work. You'd have to get it again and upload it. It's also not possible to share movies from your phone's Camera Roll or Gallery. Instead, you need to use the Uploads tab.

To remove the background from a video on your desktop computer, simply:
1. Pick out the video you want to change.
2. Click on "**Edit video**" in the window that appears on top of the editor.
3. Click "**Background Remover**" in the box on the side.
4. Please wait while the background works.

To remove the background from a video on your mobile, simply:
1. Pick out the video you want to change.
2. On the menu below the writer, press the "**Effects**" button.
3. Click on "**Background Remover**."
4. Please wait while the background works.

Using the Erase and Restore Brushes to Edit Images Created in Background Remover

These tools can only be found on canva.com and the PC app for now.

1. First, press "**Background Remover**." Then, click on the "**Erase**" or "**Restore**" brush.
2. To see or get back parts of the picture, click and drag the brush over them.
3. You can change the brush size with this tool. Click on it and drag it to the left or right to change its size.
4. To see the first picture while you're making changes, select "**Show original image**."
5. Choose "**Done**" from the tools at the top of the screen.
6. Click "**Apply**" at the bottom of the sidebar when you're done making changes.

Once you know how to use them, the Background Remover tool lets you try out different backgrounds that fit your brand and style or stand out from them. It's not enough to take your friend out of a picture for social media to get rid of the background. It's also important to make sure that the people you want to see your project can see the pictures and designs you've made.

CHAPTER 12

EXPORTING AND SHARING DESIGNS

Downloading Designs

1. Click the **Share** button ![icon] on the editor's menu bar.
2. Click **Download** ![icon].
3. From the list, pick a file type to download.
4. Choose the pages you want to download from the dropdown menu if your design has more than one. Then click "**Done**."
5. Click on **Get**.
6. To buy licensed versions of special elements in your design, click on the "**More**" icon next to "**Try Canva for Pro/Teams for free**." Pick the way of payment you want to use, then click "**Pay and Download**" to finish.

The picture you want is in the download folder that came with your device.

Supported Download File Types

Save your thoughts in the format that lets you do what you want to do with them:

Image

- **JPG.** Picture files that are small work best. Slide each one to change the size and color.
- **PNG.** It's best for images and lets you use transparency*. To change the compression ratio, check the box next to Compress file size and move the scale to 0.5x, 1x, 2x, or 3x.
- **SVG.** The picture quality stays the same no matter what size it is. It's great for making images for the web.

Users of Canva Pro, Canva Teams, Canva for Education, and Canva for Nonprofits can change the quality, the size, the compression, the CMYK color schemes, and the PNG and SVG files that are made clear.

Document

- **PDF Standard.** Up to 96 dots per inch (dpi) for pictures, text, and graphics
- **PDF Print.** For printing at 300 dpi, with the choice to choose an RGB or CMYK color scheme and add bleed and crop marks
- **PPTX (Microsoft PowerPoint).** To use only for talks. For now, downloading as PPTX is not possible for other design types.
- **DOCX (Microsoft Word).** Only works with Canva Docs. For now, you can only download DOCX for certain design types.

If you get designs as PPTX or DOCX files, they might not look the same when you open them in PowerPoint or Word. It's possible that you need to make some changes or get the fonts you used in Canva and put them on your phone. It is not yet possible to add animations and movies to Microsoft Word and PowerPoint. If you save your design as a PPTX or DOCX file, animated parts and/or movies may not work the way you want them to.

Video

- **GIF.** For designs with moving elements or those that are animated
- **MP4.** Videos and music can be used in designs

Sharing Designs via Email or Links

There are many ways to share your pictures made in Canva. You can also tell your team about your thoughts if you have or are on one.

Sharing Via Links from Inside the Editor

People can see all the comments in the editor without logging in if you give them a link to your design that only lets them see comments. Before someone can answer, add new notes, or change the plan, they have to sign up or log in.

Computer

1. Get the design you want to share and open it.
2. Pick **Share** from the menu bar above the notepad.
3. The drop-down box next to the Collaboration link lets you pick who to share with. With the link, you can share it with **All Users, Your Team** (only for Canva Teams users), or Anyone. You are the only one who can change the style that is picked by default.
4. It lets you pick which type of rights to give: can change, write, or view. You can change the rights whenever you want after that.
5. Click on **Copy link.**

Mobile

1. Open the design you want to share.
2. Tap the **Share** button above the editor.
3. Click on **Share link** .
4. You can choose who to share with by using the dropdown menu next to the **Collaboration link**. You can share with **anyone with the link, Only you can access, or Only your team (for Canva Teams users only)**. The style that is chosen by default can only be accessed by you.
5. You can choose what kind of permissions to give on the other dropdown: can change, write, or view. After this, you can change the rights whenever you want.

6. Click on **Copy link**.

Why Are There Unknown or Guest Users in My Design?

Some people with the design link can make changes if you see "guest users" in your design. These people will have animal names and pictures. No need to sign up or log in for this to let people change things.

Sharing Via Links from the Home Page

Computer

1. From the Canva home page or a folder, find the drawing you want to share.
2. Move your mouse over its picture and click the "**More**" button that shows up. You can also just click on the idea.
3. Click on **Share** .
4. You can choose who to share with by using the dropdown menu next to the Collaboration link. You can share with **All Users, Your Team (only for Canva Teams users), or Anyone with the link**. The style that is chosen by default can only be accessed by you.
5. You can choose what kind of permissions to give on the other dropdown: can change, write, or view. After this, you can change the rights whenever you want.
6. Click on **Copy link**.

Mobile

1. In Projects or your files, find the image you want to share.
2. On the image you want to share, tap the "**More**" button. You can also just click on the idea.
3. Click on **Share**.
4. You can choose who to share with by using the dropdown menu next to the Collaboration link. You can share with **All Users, Your Team (only for Canva Teams users), or Anyone with the link**. The style that is chosen by default can only be accessed by you.
5. You can choose what kind of rights to give on the other dropdown: can, edit, write, or view. After this, you can change the rights whenever you want.
6. Click on **Copy link**.

Sharing With Specific People via Email

By using their email addresses, you can let certain people see your ideas.

Computer

1. Get the design you want to share and open it.

2. Go to the menu bar in the editor after opening it. After that, click **Share** ⬆.
3. People whose emails you want to share your drawing with should be typed into the text field. There need to be commas between them. If you're on a team, you can look for their name and add them right away.
4. From the drop-down menu, you can pick whether the person can read, write, or change. You can change the rights whenever you want after that.
5. Click **Send**.

Mobile

1. Get the design you want to share and open it.
2. Click on the **Share button** at the top of the window.
3. Press the **Share** link.
4. People whose emails you want to share your drawing with should be typed into the text field. There need to be commas between them. If you're on a team, you can look for their name and add them right away.
5. From the drop-down menu, you can pick whether the person can read, write, or change. You can change the rights whenever you want after that.
6. Click "**Send**."

Sharing Profile Pictures

Users can choose from designs that have already been shared with other users. You can see who can see your design or folder if you click on your own picture.
- The only person who can see a design or place that doesn't have a picture of you is you.
- If it's shared with more than one person or team, it will have two group shots.

If the design is shared with more than two people, the second personal picture will have a "**+**" sign next to it. This means that you and at least two other people or groups can use it.

Export Print-Ready Artwork

Step 1: Create Your Artwork

Click on "**Create a Design**" in the upper right area of Canva's main screen. This is the screen you'll see: you can use a template or start from scratch with your design.

Step 2: Find the section that says "Download."

You need to share your art when you're done with your idea. Click the "**Share**" button in the top right corner of your screen. Press "**Download**."

Step 3: Change Your Export Settings

Exporting As PDFs
- Click on "**PNG**" to see the other choices. Your File Type setting is likely to be set to "**PNG**." The next step is the most important: make sure your file type is "**PDF (Print)."**
- In this case, you will get the best prints. Note: The "**crop mark**" and "**color mode**" options, as well as the output quality, are different between the **Standard and Print PDFs**. If you're giving us artwork, you don't need to make this choice because Stark doesn't use crop marks. We use flow instead.

Selecting Color Mode

They might need crop marks if you use a different printer. Talk to your printer again to find out what settings it wants you to use. The color choice is an important part of this process, though. When you print your art, it needs to be in CMYK color. The color mode for computer files like this (a blog post or a social media post) is RGB.

NOTE: You can only share your art in RGB if you use the free version of Canva. No problem, our Prepress Team can change the color mode for you. Don't forget that your work may have some small color changes. Bright colors and neons may not look as bright.

The best way to get artwork ready to print is to send it as a PDF. This way, the artwork can still be changed. Based on the graphics (images, text, or other vector graphics) in your art, you may still be able to change it with other graphic design tools.

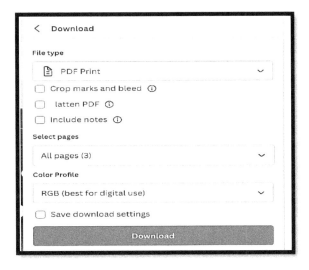

Do not check the "**Flatten PDF**" box. To make your art into a single picture, check this box in Canva. You can't change any text or graphics that were in the first version of your art. Also, if you send your art as a PDF and don't flatten it, you can still change the words. But keep in mind that some of Canva's styles are not open source, which means anyone can't use them. If we have to change your art and use that style, there may be an extra fee. No extra charge if you don't want to pay the licensing fees for the original font(s). We can always find a related font for you. When you're done setting up, there's nothing else to do! You can upload your PDF right to your payment after pressing "**Download**."

Printing Designs

1. Open the PDF file that you saved on your computer.
2. On your PDF reader, press the Print button or the printer icon. To print, you can also press **Command + P (Mac) or Ctrl + P (Windows).**
3. You can choose what kind of printer you have. Check to see if it can make the picture the size you want.
4. Check how your printer is set up. Set your picture to print at 100% scale to make sure it comes out right.
5. Press the **Print** button to print.

CHAPTER 13

TROUBLESHOOTING DESIGN ISSUES AND TIPS

Common Challenges and Solutions

1. Canva Freezing or Crashing

If Canva stops or crashes while you're working, it's probably because of your internet connection, how slow your browser is, or how complicated your design is. First, make sure you can connect to the internet. A stable network is very important for Canva to load templates, save your work, and work right. If the internet is slow, restart your computer or connect to a different network. If you're using Wi-Fi, you might want to move closer to the router to get a stronger connection. Next, clear the cache in your browser. Cached files can slow down browsers or make web apps like Canva less useful over time. Take a look at your browser's privacy settings and delete all of its cookies and cache. When you're done, restart Canva and keep working. If Canva is still slow or won't respond, close any tabs or programs that aren't needed that are running in the background. They could be using up your system's resources. Problems with compatibility can also be fixed by switching platforms. For instance, if you're having trouble with Canva in Safari, try opening it in Chrome or Edge. Any of these steps don't work? Restart your computer to get rid of any minor problems and start over. As a safety step, make your design simpler. Canva may not be able to handle large designs with a lot of high-resolution images or elements. To make the file lighter, use fewer elements or compress the pictures.

2. Image Upload Issues

Sometimes it's hard to upload pictures to Canva because of the size, format, or speed of the link. First, make sure that your picture is in a file that can be used, like PNG, JPEG, or SVG. The picture won't upload if it's in a format that isn't allowed, like RAW. You'll need to use a free tool like Convertio or a picture editor to change it to a format that works. It takes longer or doesn't work at all to upload large files. To fix this, use tools like TinyPNG to compress your picture. This will make the file smaller without losing quality. This not only makes sharing easier but also makes Canva faster overall. Check the file name if your picture still won't upload. Sometimes, special characters like "@," "#," or "&" can make it hard to share files. Change the file's name to something with easy letters and numbers. If after following these steps the file still doesn't work, open the Canva editor again. Some upload problems can also be avoided by dragging and dropping the picture right into the design. Last but not least, make sure your internet connection is strong. An unstable connection can stop downloads.

3. Fonts Not Displaying Correctly

Problems with fonts not showing up right are usually caused by font file compatibility or computer performance. Canva works with both TrueType Font (TTF) and OpenType Font (OTF) formats, so make sure that any custom fonts you post are in one of these types. If the font file type is right but the font doesn't show up, try uploading it again in Canva's Brand Kit section. The upload process doesn't always finish correctly, which leads to errors. If the fonts still don't look right, clear the cache and cookies in your browser and then reload the Canva page. It's possible for cached data to mess up the way web apps load resources like fonts. If there are display problems in a design, like writing that isn't straight, check the settings for the text box. To fix the look, change the font size, letter spacing, and line height. If these changes don't fix the problem, you might want to try a different browser to rule out problems with compatibility.

4. Alignment Issues

When things in Canva don't line up right, like text, pictures, or shapes, the design can look rough. To fix this, go to the editor's "File" menu and turn on gridlines or guides. These visual tools help you place things exactly where you want them. Canva's snap-to-grid tool will automatically line up objects with the closest guide as you move them around. This keeps everything in place. When working with several things that need to stay in the same relationship, group them together. To do this, pick all the elements you want to keep together, right-click, and choose "**Group**." This will lock their positions so you can move or resize them without losing their positions. Use the arrow keys on your keyboard to make small changes. They let you place things perfectly down to the last pixel. At times, alignment problems happen because parts are overlapping without meaning to. You can change the order of items that are stacked in Canva by using the layer controls. Send the picture to the back layer or move the text to the front if, say, a text box is hidden behind an image.

5. **Download Problems**

Problems with downloading in Canva can include downloads that don't work or files that are in the wrong format. First, make sure your internet link is stable if you can't download a design. For Canva to work and send files, it needs a stable connection. Go back to the page and try getting it again. If the download still doesn't work, make the design simpler by cutting down on the number of parts or high-resolution images that are used. It is very important to choose the right file type for downloads to work. When it comes to photos, PNG is better for high-quality pictures while JPG files are smaller. Depending on what you need, pick PDF Standard or PDF Print for your files. If some parts of the saved file are missing, make sure that all fonts, images, and other resources are loaded in the editor before you export. If you still have trouble, try a different browser or device. There are times when short-term problems with your current setup can make the download process less smooth. Last but not least, you can ask for help from Canva's support team by explaining the problem and attaching your design file.

6. **Background Remover Not Working**

Canva Pro users can use the Background Remover tool, but it doesn't always work right, especially with pictures that are complicated. If the tool doesn't get rid of the background correctly, choose a picture with a lot of contrast so that the subject and background are easy to tell apart. This helps Canva's AI figure out what to get rid of better. If the tool takes away parts of the subject, you can carefully add them back with the "Restore" brush. The "Erase" brush can help you clean up the edges if parts of the background are still there. If you're using Canva's free plan, you might want to remove the background with an outside tool like Remove.bg before importing the picture into Canva.

Tips for Saving Time

1. **Use Templates as a Starting Point**

One thing that saves me a lot of time in Canva is the templates. Start with a template that fits your design goal instead of starting from scratch. For social media posts, flyers, presentations, resumes, and more, Canva offers thousands of professionally designed templates. Use appropriate keywords to look for templates, or just browse by category. Once you find a template that works for you, change the text, pictures, and colors to make it your own. It takes less time to make plans this way, and the end result looks better.

2. **Create a Brand Kit**

Canva's Brand Kit tool can save you a lot of time if you make a lot of designs for your business or personal brand. You can put your brand's colors and images on there and save your fonts all in one place. With just a few clicks, you can add your name to any design after setting up your name Kit. For instance, when you use templates, you can quickly change the colors and styles to match your brand's settings. This way, all of your projects will look the same.

3. **Use the "Magic Resize" Tool**

It's the Magic Resize tool that changes everything for Canva Pro users. It lets you change a design to fit different sizes without starting from scratch. For example, if you design a Facebook post and then want to use the same design on Instagram or Twitter, the Magic Resize tool will change the sizes for you. It's much faster than starting from scratch, but you might need to make some small changes.

4. Save Frequently Used Elements

You can save time in Canva by using the same parts in different designs. Put images, icons, or text boxes that you use a lot in a folder that is just for them so you can get to them quickly. You can also make a design template for projects that you do over and over, like emails or social media posts, and then copy it whenever you need to. This means you don't have to redo the style or formatting each time.

5. Learn Keyboard Shortcuts

Learning how to use the computer shortcuts in Canva can make your work go much faster. As an example:

- Press **Ctrl+C** (or Command+C on Mac) to copy elements and **Ctrl+V** to paste them.
- Use **Ctrl+Z** to undo and **Ctrl+Shift+Z** to redo actions.
- Align elements quickly with **Ctrl+Arrow keys** for fine adjustments.

You will work faster if you use more shortcuts in your daily life.

6. Duplicate Designs or Pages

When making a bunch of designs that all have the same structure, like slides for a show, you don't have to start from scratch on each page. With one click, Canva lets you copy whole designs or just certain pages. This is very helpful for staying consistent and saving time on jobs that are done over and over again.

7. Use Canva's Search Function Effectively

You don't have to scroll through Canva's huge library to find elements, templates, or images. Instead, use the search bar and specific terms. You can get better results by adding filters like theme, color, or style. If you want a minimalist icon, for example, look for "minimalist" plus the type of icon (for example, "minimalist phone icon").

8. Organize Your Projects

Using folders in Canva will help you keep your designs in order. You can put jobs into groups based on types, such as client work, social media, or presentations. You'll spend less time looking for specific designs or files if you keep everything in order.

9. Use Pre-Set Dimensions

Canva has sizes already set for most projects, like Instagram posts, LinkedIn banners, and A4 papers. You can save time by choosing the right sizes from the start instead of having to change plans later. For specific uses, you can also make your own dimensions and save them for later use.

10. Collaborate in Real-Time

You can use Canva's real-time collaboration tool to help your team work on a project at the same time. When you share your design with your teammates, they can make changes or leave comments right on the design. This gets rid of the need to send and receive letters or share files, which speeds up the review process.

11. Search and Replace

The search-and-replace tool in Canva can save you time when working on designs with text that appears over and over again. You can use this tool to make changes quickly without having to edit each text box by hand if you need to change the company name or date in more than one place in your design.

12. Use Canva's Content Planner

Canva's Content Planner lets you plan posts right from the app if you are in charge of social media. This means you won't have to switch between Canva and other scheduling tools as often. You can design and schedule your content all at once.

13. **Automate Repetitive Tasks with Canva Pro**

When you upgrade to Canva Pro, you can use tools like the Background Remover and Magic Resize that can make jobs that would normally take time faster. For instance, it can be time-consuming to remove background manually, but Canva's tool does it with just one click. In the same way, Pro tools make it easy to change the size of designs for different devices.

14. **Keep Your Workspace Clean**

It will save you time in the long run to clean up your Canva desk. To make your dashboard easy to use, put away old designs or put them in folders. If you keep your work area clean, you can find what you need and start new jobs faster.

Conclusion

Canva is a powerful and user-friendly design platform that empowers both beginners and professionals to create stunning visuals with ease. By exploring its extensive range of tools, templates, and features, users can produce professional-quality designs for any purpose, from social media graphics and business cards to presentations and marketing materials. The usefulness of Canva lies in its ability to simplify the design process, making it accessible to individuals with no prior design experience while offering advanced features for seasoned creators. Its intuitive drag-and-drop interface, customizable templates, and seamless integration with other platforms ensure a smooth and efficient workflow. As you continue to explore Canva, take advantage of its features such as collaboration tools, brand kits, and animation options to elevate your designs. Experiment with elements, fonts, and layouts to discover your unique creative style. Remember, the key to mastering Canva is practice and exploring its vast resources. Whether you're designing for personal, professional, or business purposes, Canva offers the flexibility and tools to bring your ideas to life. Embrace the creativity it provides, and let your designs make a lasting impact.

INDEX

Q

R

S

U

V